EQUAL RIGHTS IS OUR MINIMUM DEMAND

THE WOMEN'S RIGHTS MOVEMENT IN IRAN, 2005

DIANA **CHILDRESS**

 TFCB TWENTY-FIRST CENTURY BOOKS ■ MINNEAPOLIS

With many thanks to Jay Barksdale and the New York Public Library for the use of its collections and the Frederick Lewis Allen Room in researching the women's movement in Iran.

Cover photo: The writing on this Iranian woman's hands reads "women should have same rights as men." The woman is at a rally in Tehran, Iran, for presidential candidate Mir-Hossein Mousavi in May 2009.

Twenty-First Century Books
A division of Lerner Publishing Group, Inc.
241 First Avenue North
Minneapolis, MN 55401 U.S.A.

Website address: www.lernerbooks.com

Library of Congress Cataloging-in-Publication Data

Childress, Diana.
    Equal rights is our minimum demand : the women's rights movement in Iran, 2005 /
by Diana Childress.
    p.   cm. — (Civil rights struggles around the world)
    Includes bibliographical references and index.
    ISBN 978–0–7613–5770–4 (lib. bdg. : alk. paper)
    1. Women's rights—Iran. 2. Women—Iran—History. 3. Muslim women—Iran. I. Title.
HQ1735.2.C485 2011
323.3′40955090511—dc22   2010028442

Manufactured in the United States of America
1 – CG – 12/31/10

CONTENTS

AN UNPRECEDENTED EVENT

On Sunday, June 12, 2005, a large crowd of women gathered on the broad plaza in front of Tehran University's main gate in Tehran, the capital of Iran. Many wore a traditional black chador, a large cloth draped loosely over the head and around the body. But most took a more relaxed view of the government requirement that women dress modestly. They covered themselves with bright red or blue jackets, loose tunics, and long print dresses. Flowered kerchiefs or multicolored scarves only partly hid their hair. Women of all ages came. Teens in fashionable oversize sunglasses, blue jeans peeking out from under long shirts, stood alongside white-haired grandmothers in full-length black robes.

The hot afternoon sun lit up the slogans on the colorful placards the women held aloft. Messages in flowing Persian script expressed angry determination. For the benefit of foreign reporters who could not read Persian, some slogans also appeared in English.

"No to legal violence against women."

"Oppressive laws and patriarchal [male-dominated] traditions should be abolished."

"Human rights are the path to democracy in Iran."

"Our path to liberation—just law and women's consciousness."

One popular poster simply used the signs scientists use to represent the female and male sexes:

$$♀ = ♂$$

The words addressed serious issues, but the mood was exuberant. Such a large turnout of women for a popular demonstration had not occurred in twenty-six years, not since the Islamic Revolution in 1979.

The event took a year to plan. In February 2004, the political party that had won control of Iran's parliament (governing body) began stripping away legal and political rights women had fought for and won. Police began arresting women's rights activists, and the government began censoring their publications (deleting passages the government objected to). Women's organizations from across Iran joined forces to demand a new constitution based on equal rights for all Iranian citizens.

Working together, the women used the Internet to reach all regions of Iran and to gain international support as well. Human Rights Watch and other rights organizations around the world became involved. Prominent women writers, professors, lawyers, artists, bloggers, and journalists helped organize the demonstration.

It was well timed. With the presidential election just five days away, the

Protesters gathered in front of Tehran University in Tehran, Iran, on June 12, 2005. These women and many others held signs and shouted their demands for women's rights in Iran.

protest gave the women a chance to direct their message to the seven male candidates. These men represented a wide range of political views. None had yet shown much interest in women's issues. The women hoped to capture their attention.

The women at the demonstration came from every social class and ethnic group and held a range of political and religious beliefs. They disagreed on how best to achieve equal rights. Some planned to vote for a candidate who had met with a group of women to hear their views, although he had made them no promises. Others believed the only course was to boycott the elections and wage a campaign to rewrite the Iranian constitution. But on this day they all put aside their differences. Waving their signs, they joined in chanting, "We are women, we are the children of this land, but we have no rights" and "Equal rights is our minimum demand."

Female members of the Iranian police (in black) attempt to stop women from joining the rally on June 12, 2005, in Tehran. The protest brought international attention to women's rights in Iran.

Security police moved in on the gathering crowd, shouting orders to leave, shoving the women, and seizing their placards. But the protesters held their ground by sitting down and crossing their arms over their heads. Seeing that the women could not be intimidated, the police surrounded the demonstrators with closely parked buses to prevent more supporters from joining them. The police also stopped hundreds of latecomers two blocks away. Refusing to disband, these demonstrators held their own, separate rally. Thousands of supporters, hecklers, and spectators filled the streets. Traffic stopped, horns honked, and tempers flared in the heat. Police had their hands full trying to stop journalists from taking photos and videos.

Meanwhile, at the university, the crowd cheered as organizers read a list of demands for "fundamental and equal rights" for women. A message from Iran's best-known women's rights activist, Nobel Peace Prize winner Shirin Ebadi, encouraged the women to keep up the struggle against "unequal treatment of half the Iranian population." Iran's best-known woman poet, Simin Behbahani, read a poem. For an hour, the women listened to speeches, sang protest songs, and enjoyed their solidarity.

Brief though it was, the demonstration was a great day for the women of Iran. For the first time, Iranian women had united to seek a common goal. They had organized a successful public demonstration and attracted international attention to their cause. Even the men running for president heard the message. The candidate of the party most opposed to women's rights, Mahmoud Ahmadinejad, began speaking against "sexist attitudes."

More important was the long-term impact. Women are still struggling for legal and political rights in Iran. But the demonstration of June 12, 2005, marked a surge in their long effort.

The story of Iran's women's movement reaches back to the days of the grandmothers and even great-grandmothers of the women who gathered in 2005. It is a story of conflict, of barriers to overcome, of successes and reversals. The movement has advanced, lost ground, and pushed ahead again. But in 2005 the women of Iran were filled with hope that they would someday overcome the obstacles keeping them from obtaining equal rights—legal, political, and cultural.

CHAPTER 1

A PATRIARCHAL PRISON

Behind the closed doors at home, prohibited from everything in life, education, training, and social life, women are regarded as mindless, like infants; they are confined to the burdens of household work and childbearing and are considered the slaves and servants of their husbands."

—Bibi Khanum Astarabadi, a performer at the Persian royal court, 1895

More than a century ago, some Iranian women were already protesting their lack of human rights. This lack arose mainly from Iran's patriarchal social system. In this system, fathers ruled in every family. Iranian culture, developed over many centuries, valued women but considered them inferior to men. Men believed they needed to protect and control women for their own good.

As guardians of the family, men took responsibility for the sexual behavior of their wives, sisters, and daughters. For a woman to have sexual relations outside marriage was a crime against her family's honor. Fathers, brothers, and husbands felt justified in killing a daughter, sister, or wife who committed such a shameful act. The government very seldom punished these so-called honor killings.

To prevent any such loss of honor, men placed many restrictions on women's lives. At home, men and male servants inhabited the part of the house closest to the street. This area was called the *biruni*. Women, children, and maids lived in the *andarun* at the back. In more modest homes, a curtain separated the male and female areas. Only men related to the women or trusted, elderly male servants could enter the women's quarters.

Upper-class women spent much of their time in the andarun with their children. Meals, games, and other family activities took place there. The visits of female relatives and door-to-door peddlers provided welcome entertainment and news of the outside world. The wealthiest households paid women performers to play musical instruments, tell religious stories, or recite Persian epics (long poems about ancient Iranian heroes).

Of course, women did at times leave the andarun. Approved outings included religious gatherings at a saint's shrine, family visits or celebrations, and baths at public bathhouses. But the women could usually go out only during the day. During the month of Ramadan, when Muslims fast from dawn until sunset, women were allowed in the streets during the evening hours, when extended families gathered to break the daily fast. Otherwise women were required to "take the sun home."

Working-class women had slightly more freedom of movement than upper-class women. Farmwomen worked outdoors in the fields. Women vendors sat in the bazaar (marketplace) behind piles of goods. Others carried farm produce or crafts to sell to well-to-do households. Women bath attendants worked in the women's public bathhouses. Domestic servants, however, lived with the families they worked for. Their lives were as confined as those of their female employers. Women weavers, seamstresses, embroiderers, and shoemakers were also housebound, working at home with their children underfoot.

Among the most independent women were midwives and healers, who cared for women in childbirth and treated women's illnesses. Women leaders of religious ceremonies, such as rituals for mourning the dead, also led professional lives. A few of these leaders gained recognition as religious scholars.

WALKING BLACK BAGS

"Half of the walking population in the streets is wrapped in black bags from head to toe without even an opening to breathe," an Iranian novelist once commented. Whatever her class, when a woman left her home, she had to wrap herself in a long, dark-colored chador. It covered her head and fell to her feet. Since the garment lacked fastenings, the wearer held it together with one hand. If she had bundles to carry or a child's hand to hold, she

This photo from 1979 shows Iranian women wearing the traditional chador. A chador is a long garment worn by some Muslim women to cover the head and body. Some women wear a full veil with the chador to cover their faces as well.

clamped the cloth between her teeth. A thin veil covered her face so that she could see out without being seen. Girls as young as nine wore chadors. At that young age, they were already eligible for marriage.

When sidewalks were crowded, women had to walk on one side of the street and men on the other. If a woman wished to reach a house or a shop on the wrong side of the street, she requested permission from a policeman to cross. The police were quick to say to any woman with her veil askew, "Cover your face, wench [prostitute]!"

Horse-drawn cabs provided public transportation, but women and men were not allowed to ride together in them. If a woman went out with her husband or her brother, they had to hire two cabs and travel separately. Men could ride in open carriages, but women could travel only in closed vehicles. Respectable married women did not go to coffeehouses or to theaters and rarely went out alone. Parents guarded unmarried girls even more closely. They did not go out alone at all.

Neither girls nor women went to school. Most men held that education was unnecessary and even dangerous for women. Some daughters in wealthy families were lucky enough to have private tutors to teach them to read Persian or Arabic or to converse in French. Broad-minded husbands and fathers might also give their wives and daughters

PERSIA/IRAN

In ancient times, Iran was known to the outside world as Persia. That is how Iran's neighbors and enemies, the Greeks, referred to the country. Iranians, however, have always referred to themselves as Iranians. In 1935 Iran's ruler, Reza Shah Pahlavi, requested that the country's name be internationally recognized as Iran, not Persia. The nation's language, however, continues to be called Persian. In the Persian language, the word for Persian is *Farsi*.

access to their libraries. However, men who allowed their women to learn to read often drew the line at writing. They feared the women would bring shame to the family by composing letters to secret lovers.

■ ■ ■ LEGAL RIGHTS

Besides being socially segregated, Iranian women had few legal rights. Many of the laws that affected women's lives came from a code of ethics called Sharia law. Sharia is based on the Quran, the holy book of Islam, and the actions and teachings of the prophet Muhammad and other important Islamic leaders. One passage in the Quran was the basis for laws requiring women to veil themselves in public. Sura (a chapter in the Quran) 24.31-32 advises both men and women to dress modestly. Moreover, it instructs women to cover their "adornments" or "ornaments" in public. Different Islamic communities interpret the words *adornments* or *ornaments* in different ways. For this reason, various forms of veiling or *hijab* exist. *Hijab* literally means "curtain," but the word is also used for women's clothing that conforms to Islamic teachings. In Iran the full coverage of the chador became customary in the late 1600s. By the 1900s, almost all Iranian women wore chadors in public. In some parts of the country, however, women practiced other forms of veiling.

Another passage in the Quran concerning women is sura 4.34. This passage states that because husbands support their wives financially, they have the right to punish wives who mismanage household funds. This sura is often cited as proof that, according to the Quran, women are subject to men. It is also used to support a husband's right to beat a disobedient wife. The idea that men must rule over women assured that Iranian women played no public or official roles in political life.

The Quran does grant women the right to own property. But inheritance laws in the Quran favor men. A daughter's share of an inheritance may be only half that of her brother's. A wife's share of her husband's estate is only one-eighth of her son's.

Not only did an Iranian woman inherit less, she was less valued as a witness in a court of law and often compensated less than a man if she was a victim of a crime. In deciding court cases, judges considered the

Islam is a monotheistic (worshipping one God) religion founded by the prophet Muhammad on the Arabian Peninsula in the seventh century A.D. The messages he received from Allah (God, in Arabic) are recorded in the Quran. Followers of Muhammad are known as Muslims. After Muhammad's death in 632, disagreement broke out over who would succeed the prophet as religious and political leader of the Muslim community. This conflict led to the division of Islam into two main sects, Sunni Islam and Shia Islam.

During the seventh century, Islam spread rapidly from Arabia to other parts of the world. Many Iranians adopted Islam when Arabs conquered most of their country in the A.D. 640s. Before that, most Iranians practiced Zoroastrianism, a monotheistic religion founded in Iran in the sixth century B.C. by the prophet Zoroaster. The Shia sect of Islam became the state religion of Iran in the sixteenth century. In the twenty-first century, about 98 percent of Iranians are Muslim. Most are Shia Muslims. About 10 percent of Iranian Muslims belong to the Sunni branch of Islam. The remaining 2 percent of Iranians are Zoroastrians, Jews, Christians, or Baha'is (followers of the Baha'i faith, founded in Iran in the nineteenth century).

testimony of one man equal to that of two women. In some situations, the law allowed equal payments to male and female victims of crimes. But in murder cases, the amount of money the perpetrator had to pay to a female victim's survivors was only half what he would have to pay if the victim was male.

■ ■ ■ ■ MARRIAGE LAWS

Marriage laws in Iran were also based on the Quran. Parents and other relatives chose husbands for their daughters. Girls could be married as young as age nine, because the prophet Muhammad had married his third wife Aisha when she was that age. This practice eased a father's worry that his teenage daughter might become sexually active before marriage. For husbands, having a young bride could reinforce the inferior status of the wife in marital relations. For the child bride, however, the experience could be horrific.

One woman who wrote about the custom of child brides in her memoirs was Taj al-Saltanah. She was a daughter of Naser al-Din Shah, who ruled Iran from 1848 to 1896. (*Shah* is the Persian word for "king.") Remembering the year she turned eight, Taj wrote, "I began to hear my nannies and my aunt frequently talk about my wedding—about how I would take a husband and how they would receive clothes and sweets. Such talk gave me immense pleasure, for I thought of unbridled freedom and a house of my own."

As the betrothal approached, however, she grew frightened. But she had no way out. "Like a captive slave . . . I was sold off to a husband whom I had not had a chance to observe and to whose character I was not accustomed," she wrote. Looking back in later years, she said sorrowfully, "Truly what greater misfortune could one suffer than to have to take a husband in childhood, at the age of eight? . . . It seems to me that in my lifetime I have lived under a cloud of misfortune and vexation [distress], all of it beginning from that ill-fated day."

Once married, a woman could not stop her husband from taking a second, third, or fourth wife. The Quran allows a man to have up to four wives at the same time, so long as he can afford to treat them equally.

Nor could wives prevent a husband from entering temporary marriages. Iranian laws allow a man to enjoy any number of temporary marriages. These relationships are arranged by a contract between a man and a woman and can last anywhere from a few hours to ninety-nine years.

Taj al-Saltanah's father married seventy wives. Her mother was a temporary wife. She and her children lived in the royal andarun

A photographer took a portrait of these mothers and daughters in an Iranian andarun in the late nineteenth century. An andarun is the secluded area in an Iranian household where women traditionally lived.

along with many of his other wives and children. Naser al-Din's marriages did not set a record. His great-grandfather wed more than one thousand women.

Not all Iranian men took multiple wives. Usually, only wealthy men married several times. Some women enjoyed having a co-wife as a companion with whom to share household chores and child-rearing. Judging from Iranian police records of the late 1800s and early 1900s, however, many household crimes resulted from friction between co-wives. Azadeh Moaveni, an Iranian American journalist, relates in her memoirs that when her great-grandfather took a second wife, her great-grandmother expressed her fury by ordering her husband's cherished mulberry orchard chopped down.

Men could divorce their wives simply by rejecting them. But for women, divorce was more difficult. Neither polygamy (marriage to more than one woman) nor wife-beating counted as grounds for divorce. A Sharia court might grant a divorce to a woman who could prove that her husband did not provide her with food and shelter.

However, she would not receive any alimony (financial support). Worse, she would lose custody of her children. By law, the custody of children of divorce went to the father or to male members of his family.

A divorced woman usually returned alone to her family. In the event of divorce, the husband was legally required to give her her dowry (a gift of money or property an Iranian man promises his bride when they marry). Few divorced women, however, managed to collect it. A divorcée was free to remarry. She might have a greater role in choosing her second husband, but men usually preferred younger women who had not married before. If she was poor, she might have to settle for a temporary marriage.

> **"Persian women have been set aside from humankind. . . . They live their entire lives of desperation in prison, crushed under the weight of bitter ordeals."**
>
> —*Taj al-Saltanah, daughter of Iranian ruler Naser al-Din Shah, 1914*

▉ ▉ ▉ WESTERN INFLUENCES

By the mid-nineteenth century, the harnessing of steam power and the invention of new machines had enabled European countries to build industries and improve transportation and communication. With the growth in production, European merchants wanted to expand trade to less industrially developed areas. There they could sell manufactured goods and buy raw materials. Russia and Great Britain were especially attracted to Iran's cotton, silk, tobacco, and oil.

Naser al-Din was eager to become trading partners with the West and to modernize Iran. By selling mining rights and the right to build factories to foreign businesses, the shah acquired the funds to build roads, set up telegraph lines, and create a postal service.

His most important investment was in education. The Dar al-Fonun (Abode of Learning) school, founded in 1852, trained aristocratic young men for government service. The best students won scholarships to study abroad in France or Belgium. The shah built other schools that specialized in agriculture, political science, foreign languages, and military training.

The shah also allowed missionaries (religious teachers) to open schools for Iran's non-Islamic minorities, then about 5 percent of the population. Christian groups from the United States, France, and Britain, a French Jewish organization, and a Zoroastrian (a native Persian religion) community from India opened schools for the children of their religious groups, including girls. But no one provided schools for Iran's Muslim girls and women.

Iranian daughters often envied the advantages their brothers enjoyed. They saw women missionaries from the United States and the wives of European businessmen and diplomats wearing stylish dresses in the streets. They heard about suffragettes marching in London, England, and Paris, France, demanding the right to vote in elections and to be included in government affairs. "They are winning successes," Taj wrote in 1914 about women activists in the West. "In America their rights are fully established," she claimed, unaware that most women in the United States did not yet have the right to vote.

Taj and many other Iranian women were tired of their secluded lives and limited choices. They wanted the freedom and rights women enjoyed elsewhere.

CHAPTER 2

IRANIAN WOMEN MARCH FORTH

"Are we not, the oppressed female population of Iran, human beings as yourselves? Are we not partners and participants in the general rights of humanity with you? Do you only consider us voiceless, and load-carrying animals, or do you also recognize us as human beings? We ask for your sense of justice."

—An open letter to theology (religion) students from "the supporters of education for the oppressed women of Iran," March 22, 1908

At the beginning of the twentieth century, upper-class Iranian women began to assert themselves. They were inspired by Western women in their midst and accounts of women's movements in the newspapers. Some of their husbands, brothers, and fathers encouraged their independence. While traveling and studying in Europe, upper-class Iranian men had become accustomed to men and women mixing socially and women having public lives. Education abroad also opened their eyes to other, more representative forms of government and such modern conveniences as railroads and indoor plumbing.

Meanwhile, opposition to the shah was growing. A major sore point was Naser al-Din's sale of trade rights to foreign businessmen. Russians had purchased fishing rights on the Caspian Sea to the north. The British had gained rights to oil in southern Iran. As much as they

admired the West, the educated classes in Iran did not want Europeans to take over Iran. They worried Iran would become a European colony like nearby British India.

Merchants and artisans took issue with the shah because his economic policies hurt their businesses. Religious leaders, for their part, disliked the foreigners for bringing Western ideas and lifestyles to Iran. They wanted to protect Iran's traditional culture from changes they considered immoral.

In 1891, when the shah sold a British company the right to process and sell the entire Iranian tobacco crop, Iranians poured out into the streets to object. A tobacco boycott spread across the nation. People refused to buy tobacco and picketed merchants selling it. Joining the demonstrations, groups of women invaded shops that were not observing the boycott and forced them to close.

Even the shah's wives in the royal andarun took part in the protest. Smashing their glass water pipes, they refused to join the shah for his after-dinner smoke. The shah backed down and canceled the contract. It was the first sign that an organized revolt might lead to a new form of government for Iran.

THE CONSTITUTIONAL REVOLUTION OF 1906

In 1896 a man opposed to the shah, acting alone, assassinated Naser al-Din. Naser's son Muzaffar al-Din became shah. Needing money, the new shah continued to make unpopular foreign business deals. Unhappy Iranians formed secret societies to discuss what to do. They were not prepared to overthrow the shah. What they wanted was a better organized, more just, and more representative government. They wanted a constitutional monarchy like those in place in Britain, Belgium, and various other European nations. The shah would remain head of state, but an elected body of legislators would pass laws, government agencies would put them into practice, and an independent court system would review them. It seemed the perfect solution. The educated class, the merchants and artisans, and the clergy (religious leaders) banded together under the banner of constitutionalism.

Muzaffar al-Din became shah of Persia in 1896. He is shown here in 1899.

Women excitedly added their voices to the movement. "The light of law has opened our eyes and hearts," one woman wrote to a newspaper. "The torch of humanity is in our hands. Now that we have set ourselves on this path, you will witness how women will set alight a flaming fire in this country with the torch of humanity."

In 1905, after a bad harvest and a cholera epidemic that disrupted trade, the prices of wheat, sugar, and other staple foods soared. The crisis provoked violent protests in Tehran. Women as well as men took part in the demonstrations. The shah sent his police and troops to stop the rioting. A number of religious leaders who had encouraged the protests gathered in a shrine, where they thought they would be safe. When the shah nevertheless ordered the army to attack the shrine, women on the roof of the shrine threw rocks down on the soldiers.

The event marked the beginning of a popular revolution in which women played an active role. They were not afraid to appeal directly to the shah. On one occasion, a crowd of women surrounded the shah's carriage in the streets, demanding he stop persecuting the clergy. They threatened rebellion if the shah asked for foreign help. "If Russia and England come to your support," they warned the shah, "upon [the clergy's] command, millions of Iranians will declare jihad!" Jihad means "religious struggle." In this case, it meant that it would be Iranians' religious duty to oppose the shah.

Women also sent letters to the shah. One carried the menacing message, "Fear the time when we shall finally take away the crown off your head." Another letter, from the women's revolutionary committee, came decorated with a red hand wielding a pistol. The letter threatened the shah with death if he did not meet the rebels' demands.

Anger at the shah grew, and protests spread from Tehran to other towns. In mid-1905 the shah's forces shot a young clergyman. Huge crowds turned out to mourn him. Women marched through Tehran wrapped in shrouds, like corpses, to show their readiness to die in the revolution.

Fearing arrest, rebel leaders went to the British Embassy. By international law, a country's embassy is considered part of that country. The army or police of the host country may not enter it without permission. More than twelve thousand supporters joined the rebel leaders, their tents crowded into the embassy's garden. Several thousand women begged to join the massive gathering, but the leaders refused. The women organized protests at other sites and supported the rebels with food and money. Meanwhile, the rebels demanded that the shah agree to a constitutional government for Iran.

After a three-week standoff, in August 1906 the shah gave in. He allowed Iranians to elect an assembly to draft a constitution. In December the assembly presented the Fundamental Law, based on the Belgian constitution, to Muzaffar al-Din. This constitution established an elected National Consultative Assembly to initiate and write laws. A Senate, half of its members appointed by the shah and half elected by male citizens, would approve the laws proposed by the assembly or request amendments. The shah signed the constitution on December 3. He died of a heart attack a few days later.

■ ■ ■ ■ WOMEN WORK TO BUILD IRAN

Muzaffar's son and successor, Muhammad Ali Shah, was not happy with his father's surrender. But at first he was powerless to oppose it. The newly elected assembly, known as the Majlis, began debating legislation.

Women wholeheartedly supported the new regime, hoping to gain a role in it. They organized many women's associations and set to work forging a democratic nation. Their first priority was education. A few Muslim girls had already begun to attend a girls' school run by American Presbyterian missionaries. A French convert to Islam had opened a school for his daughters and other girls in their neighborhood. In 1907 a Muslim woman founded the first school for Muslim girls. Other schools soon followed. None of the schools received any subsidies from the Majlis, because high-ranking clerics (members of the clergy) convinced lawmakers that girls did not need schooling.

Denied public support, women found other funding sources. Wealthy women donated their own money. Women's groups held garden parties and put on plays to raise cash. One women's group proposed to abolish "onerous [burdensome] dowries" to free up funds for education.

By 1910 more than fifty schools for girls had been established in Tehran. Many of the clergy denounced the schools as contrary to Islamic law. Coming and going from their classes, female students and teachers dodged insults and stones thrown by angry conservatives. A few schools had to close, but others opened. Girls' education could not be stopped.

Women's organizations took up many other social causes as well. The members of the National Ladies Society, founded in 1910, displayed their opposition to Iran's dependence on foreign trade by only wearing dresses of Iran-made cloth. They also opened a home and a school for one hundred orphan girls. The school's director was Christian, but she wore a chador so that Muslim girls would be allowed to attend. Other groups opened health clinics and taught illiterate women to read.

When the Majlis voted to establish a national bank, women backed the effort. Wealthy women sold their jewels to buy shares in the new institution. One heiress donated five thousand tumans (a former Iranian currency). Women of more modest means contributed what they could. "Why should the government borrow from foreigners?" one woman asked a group of women gathered at a mosque (Islamic house of worship). "Are we dead? I am a laundress and can contribute my share of one tuman. Other women are ready to contribute too."

In the early 1900s, Mahrukh Gawharshinas joined a revolutionary women's association. All members of the group vowed to make a lifetime commitment to women's liberation. They each wore a special ring with clasped hands, marking their solidarity. Although Gawharshinas lacked an education, she decided to open a girls' school in Tehran in 1911.

She kept the school secret from her husband because he believed women should not be educated. She managed to conceal the school from him for two years. When her husband finally found out what she was doing, he accused her of forsaking all "religion and virtue." His main concern was the shame and disgrace her activities would bring on the family. That did not stop her.

True to her vow, she kept the school open. Not only that, she allowed boys to attend as well. When she added a high school, she invited distinguished scholars to teach. The school became so respected that a leading Muslim scholar sent his daughter there. One alumna, later a distinguished lawyer, praised her former principal as "a model of the perfect woman."

CIVIL WAR

The constitutionalists soon splintered into factions (separate groups). Merchants and artisans backed the economic goals of the movement, but opposed the liberation of women from their traditional roles. They and the clergy wanted an Islamic government overseen by religious scholars. Many of the educated elite, on the other hand, believed in the separation of mosque and state. Heated debates in the Majlis slowed the drafting of a bill of rights for the constitution. One influential religious leader broke with the new government when the Majlis voted to give non-Muslim men full citizenship.

The Majlis deputies (as the members are called) largely avoided "the woman question." Most of the clergy, whom the women had fiercely defended during the revolution, now wanted them back in the andarun, keeping house and raising children. The merchants shared their conservative views. Women activists grew impatient at the politicians' neglect of their rights. In a letter to a newspaper, one woman asked for an explanation. "Why is it that the Constitution has prevented women from gaining their rights? Women did not take part in the revolution to have their rights trampled upon."

It was not easy to get the Majlis to bother about women's concerns. Even men who supported giving women more rights thought that other issues needed attention first.

The most serious threat was war. In 1907 the British and the Russians signed an agreement to carve Iran into "spheres of influence" (areas of economic control). The shah, bolstered by generous loans from the Russians, allowed the Russians to move troops into Iran's northern provinces. With this Russian support, he decided it was time to overthrow the constitutionalists and restore absolute rule. In June 1908, he swiftly took control of the army, put soldiers in charge of law enforcement, and sent troops to bombard the Majlis building. Many deputies escaped to Tabriz, a city in northern Iran, but several were captured and executed.

In the civil war (1907–1909) that followed, many women came to the defense of the constitution. When the royalist army laid siege to Tabriz, veiled women guarded barricades in the streets. A special women's battalion fought side by side with the men.

Some individual women joined the troops disguised as men. Men clearing battlefields after battles or skirmishes discovered women's bodies dressed in men's clothing and armed with weapons. One wounded soldier refused medical treatment because she did not want her rescuers to discover her sex.

The number of women who took part in the war is not known. One scholar estimates that they numbered in the thousands. Many came from the upper classes—the daughters and wives of aristocrats, clergy, and members of the Majlis—but working-class women also volunteered. "According to witnesses," one historian wrote later, the women warriors "showed exceptional courage and devotion to duty."

In 1909 volunteer armies captured the shah in Tehran. He agreed to abdicate (give up his right to rule) and go into exile (live outside of Iran). His twelve-year-old son Ahmad became the next shah. Constitutional rule returned to Iran.

STILL NO POLITICAL ROLE FOR WOMEN

Women once again petitioned for more rights. But Iran was not yet ready for women to vote or to serve in public office. When the new Majlis discussed electoral issues in August 1911, one deputy dared to bring up the subject of woman suffrage (right to vote). Women, like men, are human beings, he said. There is no rational motive for excluding them from the vote. He called on a leading cleric to support him. But the cleric replied, "God has not given [women] the capacity to be electors. Their powers of judgment are lacking. . . . As God has said in the Qur'an, women are in the custody of men and they may not have the right to vote."

Women did not give up. There was still a long path ahead, but they were not about to withdraw to the andarun. They saw constitutional government as their best hope for eventually gaining their rights. They were still ready to defend it by every means available to them.

WOMEN RESPOND TO THE RUSSIAN THREAT

In November 1911, Iran again faced the threat of a Russian invasion. Britain backed the Russian threat. Both nations demanded that Iran stop taxing the profits of their businesses in Iran. They also called for the ouster of Iran's finance minister, an American financier. All across the nation, Iranians poured into streets. About fifty thousand people

Russian troops line up in Iran in 1911. The Russians, backed by Britain, wanted to ease restrictions on foreign trade. People across Iran, including women, protested the government giving in to Russian demands.

marched in Tehran. A general strike closed down markets, industries, and transportation. Women helped enforce a boycott on all Russian and British products and services. They stopped British-run streetcars and persuaded passengers to get out, even offering to pay for other, Iranian-owned transportation. They demanded that coffeeshops serving imported sugar shut down.

On December 1, thousands of women assembled in front of the Majlis. Many again wore white shrouds. In fiery speeches they urged the Majlis not to give in to Russia and Britain. Amin Zainab, a founding member of the National Ladies Society and a teacher at a girls' school, read a stirring poem she had written for the occasion.

> Death is better than life without honor!
> Let us fight like lions, like heroes
> Let us adorn this age with good repute!
> Now is the time for action! Be brave!

Her audience responded with cries of "Independence or death!"

Patriotic fervor spread. The shah and his army advised surrender to the Russians. The Majlis stalled in heated debate, unable to reach agreement. Women penned newspaper editorials and sent telegrams to foreign governments to ask for aid. They challenged the Majlis to oust the Russians from Iran's northern border. At mass meetings in mosques, in the area curtained off for women, they preached Iranian independence.

On one occasion, three hundred chador-clad women marched on the Majlis. The speaker of the Majlis agreed to meet with a delegation of them. Once inside, the women drew out revolvers hidden in their sleeves and pulled aside the white veils covering their faces. They declared that they would kill their husbands, their sons, and themselves if the Majlis did not preserve the liberty of the Iranian people. They left copies of their speeches behind for the deputies to read. One Majlis deputy commented, "The women teach us how to love our country."

But Iran did not stand a chance against Russia and Britain. In late December, the Iranian prime minister and the cabinet (the heads of government departments) overthrew the Majlis and gave in to the Russian demands. The struggle to establish a government based on laws agreed to by elected representatives of the people had failed. The Constitutional Revolution was over. The women's movement was not.

During these tumultuous times, the seeds of Iranian feminism took root. Women gained little ground legally and politically, but they learned to organize and to speak their minds openly in public. They made a crack in the education barrier. Most of all, they made their presence felt in the effort to bring rule of law to Iran.

> "Behind the veil out of doors, behind the curtain indoors, left out of every social function, public or private, in which men play any part, [the women of Iran] are seldom educated, trusted, valued or respected. How can a country progress with its womanhood handicapped to this extent?"
>
> —Clara Rice, wife of a British representative in Tehran, 1923

Women's associations in Iran often met secretly to avoid harassment from those who opposed women's rights. The Women's Freedom Society met twice a month in a garden outside Tehran. Taj al-Saltanah was among its sixty women members. Women attended meetings with their husbands or other male relatives. No unescorted women or single men were allowed, and only women were permitted to lecture or join the discussion. The idea was to help them get used to speaking in front of men they were not related to. Gradually these sheltered ladies learned to assert their opinions on women's issues and the problems of family life.

One evening an unaccompanied man asked to attend a meeting. When he was turned down, he reported the group to conservative clergy in downtown Tehran. An angry mob, waving sticks and shouting, paraded out to the garden where the group met. A young man sympathetic to the women's movement saw what was happening. He jumped on his bicycle and pedaled out ahead of the rabble to warn the group. Society members fled and hid, escaping the attack.

A few women, among them Taj al-Saltanah, raised questions about marriage and divorce laws, polygamy, women's legal rights, veiling, the vote and the right to run for office, and gender equality. But these were not yet the focus of a real women's movement. Iranian women still lacked a nationwide organization, a large popular following, and a platform clearly stating their goals. Although some working-class women had participated in the revolution, most women activists belonged to the educated upper classes. They could rouse women to action for a patriotic cause but not as yet for themselves. The struggle for women's liberation in Iran had just begun.

CHAPTER 3

THE GREAT AWAKENING

> "I take up the pen to complain greatly about fathers and husbands of Iranian girls. Why do they not know yet that woman and man in this world are like the two wheels of a carriage, that they must be equal, neither having any privilege over the other? If one of the two wheels of a carriage is deficient, it will be impossible for it to move."

—Shahnaz Azad, in a letter to the women's magazine *Shukufah*, January 20, 1916

Political turmoil continued to engulf Iran after 1911. In spite of the political unrest, Iranian women kept fighting for rights. It wasn't easy. Both social and political pressures conspired to limit women's public lives. Yet women who had tasted a more active public role during the revolution refused to retreat. Some had constitutionalist husbands and fathers who encouraged their efforts. Others had to defy their families. Almost all of them belonged to the upper class and lived in Tehran and other large cities. But they wanted to spread the message and bring freedom to all of Iran's women.

A SURGE IN GIRLS' SCHOOLS

Education remained a priority. The number of private schools for girls grew. Women's organizations and individual women and men founded and funded the schools. For them, girls' education was a mission. They saw educated women as the cornerstone of a strong and independent nation.

Wealthy families supported the schools with the fees they paid for their daughters' education. The money helped pay for poorer girls who could not otherwise afford to go to school. School directors charged tuition according to a family's ability to pay. Some girls received discounts. Others paid nothing at all. Often a quarter to a half of the student body received some form of financial aid. A few schools even had more scholarship students than students paying full tuition.

By 1913 an estimated 2,475 girls were enrolled in sixty-three schools in Tehran. This was not a large number, considering that about two hundred fifty thousand people lived in the city in the early 1900s. But even that number of female students created a scarcity of teachers. Few women were educated enough to teach. Some school directors recruited retired male teachers to fill the gap. Old men, they reasoned, were less likely to worry the clergy and girls' parents. Schools with an all-female faculty advertised the fact.

In 1918 the government opened a teachers' training college for women in Tehran with elderly men as teachers. One was blind. At least in his class students didn't have to cover their faces with veils.

Among the first thirty students was fourteen-year-old Badr ol-Muluk Bamdad. The daughter of a constitutionalist activist, she had received her elementary education at home. When she earned her teaching certificate, the Ministry of Education rewarded her with a Quran for being the best student. Soon after graduation, still a teenager, she became the first woman in Iran to write a textbook. For her, the college marked the start of a career in education, writing, and the strong promotion of women's rights.

Also in 1918, Sediqeh Dowlatabadi, a member of the National Ladies Society during the revolution, opened the first girls' school in Esfahan. This conservative stronghold is 200 miles (320 kilometers) south of Tehran. Like Bamdad, Dowlatabadi had been homeschooled by tutors, but she had also attended her brothers' school, disguised as a boy.

The school in Esfahan school did not last long. Angry mobs attacked the school and beat Dowlatabadi. City authorities decided to close the school down three months after it opened. They ordered the arrest of a friend of Dowlatabadi who was directing the school.

In 1919 girls' schools finally won official recognition from the Ministry of Education. At the end of that year, for the first time, all primary school graduates, boys and girls, received a diploma from the state. But in spite of its show of interest, the government budgeted little money to start public schools for girls, and girls' education stayed mainly in private hands.

Girls' schools still faced opposition from traditionalists, even in Tehran, the site of most of the schools. Bamdad wrote that neighborhood thugs often attacked her and her classmates as they came and went from the Women's Teacher Training College. But they held their ground: "On several occasions the girls beat these youths on the head with thick books which they pulled out from under their chadors."

■ WOMEN'S VOICES IN PRINT

During the Constitutional Revolution, hundreds of new periodicals hit the newsstands. They represented a range of views, liberal to conservative. Many of these new publications printed women's letters, giving women a chance to express themselves in writing. Some newspapers also published longer essays written by women about women's liberation.

The first Iranian magazine edited by a woman, *Danesh* (Knowledge), appeared in Tehran in 1910. Two years later, *Shukufah* (Blossom), edited and published by a woman, began publication. Both magazines aimed to raise women's awareness of their need for more education. Articles discussed such topics as the disadvantages of early marriage and the dangers of superstitions.

After her school closed, Sediqeh Dowlatabadi started the Women's Organization of Esfahan and a newspaper called *Zaban-e Zanan* (Women's Voice). In her first editorial, she wrote that the newspaper's intent was "to challenge the backwardness and feeble-mindedness of Esfahan" concerning women.

Published weekly, the paper carried articles addressing women's issues as well as politics. It also had an activist side. The paper helped women start small weaving workshops that employed only women. The goal was to help them gain economic independence.

The newspaper's outspokenness attracted government searches and public insults. When Dowlatabadi dared to criticize the chador, she received threats against her life. She refused to be cowed. "If they [the government and the public] want us [to] stop enlightening the public," she wrote in an editorial, "if they think we are frightened, if they wish us to block our writings and cover up the truth, if they think they can force us to lie or to forget Iran, . . . they are wrong. They live in a world of dreams and hallucination."

After two years of publication, *Zaban-e Zanan* was selling twenty-five hundred copies a week and gaining more men readers than women. But when Dowlatabadi took aim against British political influence in Iran, the government banned further publication. "Madam," Esfahan's police chief wrote to Dowlatabadi, "you are born 100 years too soon." She wrote him back: "Sir, I am born 100 years too late; otherwise, I would not have permitted our women to be chained so viciously and violently by you men." Dowlatabadi gave up on Esfahan, but not on herself or on women's rights in Iran. In 1920 she packed up and went to Paris, France, to further her education.

More women's periodicals appeared in 1920. Shahnaz Azad edited *Nameh-ye Banovan* (Women's Letter), with the motto "This newspaper is for the awakening of the suffering Iranian women." Both she and her husband suffered plenty for publishing it. Over the years, they faced a number of arrests, imprisonments, and even exiles for printing articles the government found objectionable.

Also in 1920, the alumnae association of the American Girls' School (originally the Presbyterian missionary school) started *Alam-e Nesvan* (Women's Universe). Its articles focused chiefly on women's health issues and household hints. A few tackled more controversial topics. One criticized the chador, but in a humorous way. "Our difference with foreign [Western] women," it stated, "is that when they leave their house, their teeth are not working; they only use their two hands. But we, poor creatures, have to hold our chador, the sign of our honor, with our teeth and hold our belongings with our hands. It is clear how we look in this situation. During the winter, when our nose is running, we should call someone to blow it for us. And this is the ridiculous fashion with which we step outside. Thank God nobody can recognize us."

In 1921 Afaq Parsa dared to start her magazine *Jahan Zanan* (Women's

Iranian women in chadors and veils walk along a street in Tabriz, Iran, in 1920. A humorous article in *Women's Universe* in 1920 criticized the chador.

World) in conservative Mashhad. This city, about 450 miles (720 km) east of Tehran, is home to a major Islamic shrine and a center for Islamic scholars. At first, Parsa limited articles to relatively safe topics such as women's education. An editorial critical of veiling, however, brought violent attacks. A mob looted her home. Exiled to Tehran, she resumed publication of *Women's World* only to encounter more opposition. A conservative cleric called her an enemy of Islam. Closing the magazine, she and her family finally settled in the city of Qom.

■ ■ ■ THE PATRIOTIC WOMEN'S LEAGUE

Women's organizations continued to play an important role in the feminist movement. The movement organized activities on behalf of women's rights and interests. Like earlier women's organizations, they often met secretly. Yet they managed to spread the message of women's rights through both publications and community outreach projects.

Mohtaram Eskandari, the daughter of a prince (a son or male descendant of a shah), was one of many women unhappy that the Constitutional Revolution had achieved so little for women. She decided to channel her frustration into political action. In 1922 she and several like-minded friends founded the Patriotic Women's League (PWL). It too published a magazine. But its greatest impact came from directly appealing to women and girls by giving speeches at school celebrations and private parties and holding public demonstrations.

In one bold event, PWL members, led by Eskandari, collected religious pamphlets warning men against women's wiles (trickery). The members burned them in a public square. The police hauled the women off to the station. Eskandari was not intimidated. "We did it to defend the honor of your mothers and sisters," she told the officers. "We are rational and intelligent like all human beings, but we are not wily." The police officers ended up on the women's side and let the group go.

The PWL also taught uneducated women to read and write. To raise money for the classes, the women staged plays and showed movies in private homes. Women flocked to these events, since only men were allowed to go to public theaters and movie houses.

■ ■ ■ A NEW DYNASTY
TAKES OVER

Meanwhile, Iran was undergoing a major political upheaval. In 1921 an ambitious colonel, Reza Khan, overthrew the weak government in Tehran. He assured the shah he was saving the monarchy from a Russian takeover.

Over the next two years, Reza Khan rose first to commander-in-chief of the army, then to war minister, and then to prime minister. At that point, Ahmad Shah left Iran for a holiday in Europe, perhaps aware he might never return. Reza Khan briefly considered making Iran a republic (in this case, a form of government with a head of state who is not a monarch), with himself as president. But religious

Reza Shah Pahlavi is pictured with three of his children—*(left to right)* Crown Prince Mohammad Reza, Princess Shams, and Princess Ashraf— in this undated photo. He overthrew Iran's government in 1921 and crowned himself shah in 1926.

leaders, worried that secular (nonreligious) law courts would replace Sharia law, opposed the idea. To gain their support, Reza Khan decided to retain the monarchy. He forced the Majlis to depose Ahmad and vote himself shah. On April 25, 1926, dressed in a jewel-studded outfit, he crowned himself Reza Shah Pahlavi. Pahlavi, the name he chose for his new dynasty, is an early Iranian language spoken from the third century B.C. to the third century A.D.

Once crowned, with a strong and loyal army to back him, Reza Shah marched ahead with plans to modernize Iran. He united the nation by building roads and railways and creating a central bureaucracy to run it. He took control of the economy, regulated foreign trade, and promoted industrialization. He increased the number of public schools for both boys and girls. Except for laws concerning family matters, he had the government draft new, secular laws that were based on European models.

Not all of Reza Shah's innovations aided or appealed to all Iranians. Religious leaders in particular felt sidelined as their role diminished. Schools, civil and criminal law courts, and government offices, once run largely by clergy, came under the authority of secular government departments.

In December 1928, Reza Shah ordered all urban males except religious scholars and students to wear Western-style suits and hats. Tailors and hatters welcomed the rule. Religious Muslim men, however, objected to what came to be called the Pahlavi cap. Styled after French military headwear, the cylindrical cap had a brim at the front. One could not pray properly wearing such a hat, men complained. The brim did not allow the wearer's forehead to touch the ground as is required in Muslim prayer.

CO-OPTING THE WOMEN'S MOVEMENT

Women's rights activists hoped the new shah would include them in his sweeping innovations. The Patriotic Women's League pressed for equal pay for working women and reform of marriage, divorce, and inheritance laws. Sediqeh Dowlatabadi returned from Paris and Afaq Parsa left Qom to add their voices to the PWL in Tehran. The younger generation was also becoming involved with women's rights. Zandokht Shirazi formed the Association of Revolutionary Women in 1927, when she was only eighteen. More radical than the PWLers, she set her heart on nothing short of equal rights for women.

Reza Shah responded by inviting the president of the PWL to help organize an international conference on women's issues to be held in Tehran in December 1932. As honorary chair of the conference, however, he selected not an activist but his thirteen-year-old daughter, Princess Ashraf.

Delegates from Lebanon, Egypt, Iraq, Turkey, India, and ten other Middle Eastern and Asian countries attended the conference. In their discussions, they deplored the status of women in their countries. They adopted an array of resolutions that included woman suffrage; equal opportunity for women in education, jobs, and wages; new family laws; and an end to polygamy and prostitution.

These ambitious goals, however, were not on Reza Shah's agenda. He wanted Iran to be a modern, world-class nation and knew that women must play an active role in it. But he was not prepared to go as far as granting women the vote or equal rights. His solution: take over the women's movement. This action fit with everything else he was doing in Iran—banning labor unions, amending the constitution to increase his power and reduce that of the Majlis, suppressing political parties that opposed the monarchy, and censoring the press.

In 1935 the shah called on a group of educated women, among them Badr Bamdad, to form a Ladies' Center. Funded by the Ministry of Culture and Islamic Guidance, the Ladies' Center would take over much of the work women's associations had been doing to educate and train poor women. But it limited the subjects educated women could teach their poorer sisters. Literacy, hygiene, modern methods of child care, yes. Voting, equal rights, and other feminist (women's rights) issues, no. The honorary president of the Ladies' Center was to be Her Imperial Highness Shams Pahlavi, the shah's eighteen-year-old daughter.

The women had little choice but to comply. The shah had banned all private women's associations and shut down their periodicals. Their only chance of having any public role was to teach or to become involved with the Ladies' Center.

Besides, women who believed in women's liberation saw several pluses in Reza Shah's regime. For one thing, he promoted girls' education. Public schools for girls were spreading rapidly. In 1929, 190 schools enrolled 11,489 girls. By 1933 Iran had 870 girls' elementary and high schools, most of them public, with as many as 45,000 students. In 1935, after opening Iran's first university, the shah announced that women would be allowed to apply the following year. Bamdad was one of twelve lucky women admitted in 1936.

A second advantage was that the shah had begun to relax Iran's separation by gender. At last, men and women could be seen together in public. They could go to restaurants, movies, plays, and parks together. They could even ride in carriages together—so long as the hood was down. When the shah held teas for government officials, he required them to bring their wives. For feminists, especially women like Dowlatabadi, who was used to mixed social gatherings in France, all this was welcome news. (For women who had never mixed socially with men not related to them, the idea was terrifying.)

A third reason women activists were willing to work with Reza Shah was that he wanted the Ladies' Center to prepare Iranian women for unveiling. Many feminists longed to dispense with veils and chadors. Although the lack of political and legal rights was a more pressing issue, they believed that veiling symbolized women's low status in Iran. Most women activists applauded unveiling as a step in the right direction.

The Ladies' Center, however, shifted the focus of the women's movement. Motherhood, home economics, and liberal arts education replaced women's rights as areas of concern. Yet Dowlatabadi accepted the directorship of this weakened organization. She no doubt saw it as a platform for further efforts on behalf of women. Many activists joined her, among them Bamdad and Parsa. Some saw Reza Shah as a white knight rescuing women from prison. Others felt that working with the dictator was not ideal but was better than retreat.

"A GREAT DAY"

Soon after the start of the Ladies' Center came the landmark event that shocked everyone. On January 7, 1936, at the graduation ceremonies of the Women's Teacher Training College, Queen Taj (the shah's wife) and her two daughters appeared on the platform. They wore European dresses and hats, their faces uncovered for all to see. In the audience sat all of the women teachers in Tehran. They too were unveiled, having received orders to not to wear chadors. It was Reza Shah's dramatic way of announcing his next move: declaring the veil illegal.

Years later, Bamdad recalled "the looks of astonished disbelief on the faces of the men in the streets and the crowds lining the royal route, when they saw some schoolmistresses walking by unveiled." Many in the auditorium applauded the bare-faced royal ladies as

Reza Shah married four times. The first was a temporary marriage that ended before he became shah. He supported a daughter from that marriage. The other three were permanent marriages. Taj ol-Moluk, the mother of Reza Shah's heir and successor, Mohammad Reza Shah Pahlavi, was his second wife. She became his queen and lived with her four children in the old, official Golestan Palace in Tehran. He divorced his aristocratic third wife. His fourth wife, Esmat Dowlatshahi, another aristocrat, became his favorite. She and her children lived with the shah in the new Marble Palace. Queen Taj admitted in her memoirs, "Like all other women, I hated my co-wife."

"pioneers of women's freedom." But some of the elderly female teachers, "upset by the loss of facial cover," stood "looking at the wall and perspiring with embarrassment."

After Queen Taj handed out the diplomas, Reza Shah took the podium. "You ladies should consider this as a great day," he said. He believed the new policy was good business for Iran because it showed Iran was a modern country. "You should avail yourselves of the opportunities which you now have to improve your country," he told the women. "It is my firm belief that in order to bring progress and prosperity to our own country we should all work and work wholeheartedly. . . . The future happiness of the country is in your hands."

The abrupt change in the law did not please all. For many women, the adjustment was hard. Going out without a chador felt like going out naked. In her 2009 memoir, the Iranian scholar Haleh Esfandiari wrote that her grandmother "stayed home for five years rather than go out into the street unveiled," adding that her reaction was "not uncommon."[10]

To make matters worse, the law was strictly enforced. Police who once scolded women for not covering enough now snatched off veils and chadors. "I saw it happen with my own eyes," a woman who was ten at the time recalled. "They ripped scarves off women's heads, even in Tehran."

Reza Shah ordered cafés, restaurants, theaters, and buses to stop veiled women from entering. He also dismissed government workers who did not bring unveiled wives to official functions. Women who worked for the government lost their jobs if they showed up wearing veils. Veiled women could not receive care at public health clinics or diplomas when they completed school. In Tabriz, two young women from conservative families were denied the first and second honors they had earned because they would not come to the graduation exercises unveiled. To many, this was "not women's emancipation [liberation] but police repression."

RESISTING UNVEILING

Iranian women who refused to unveil had a hard time going out. One woman recruited her grown son to carry her in a sack to the bathhouse every week. One day a policeman stopped the young man to ask what he had in his bag.

"Pistachios," the man replied.

"Let me have some," said the policeman.

As he reached for the bag to help the man put it down to open it, his hands tickled the woman inside. Giggles erupted inside the bag, and the trick was exposed. The woman wriggled out of the sack and ran off. The policeman arrested the man.

> "A group of people, including myself, believe that removal of the chador will not create freedom, nor will hijab prevent moral corruption. Is [being able to go] to the movies and theater . . . the only purpose of removing the chador?"
>
> —Fatemeh Ansari, writing in the magazine Alam-e Nesvan (*Women's Universe*), 1932

OTHER GAINS FOR WOMEN

Besides education, the shah focused on improving the health of Iranians. One pet project was to increase physical education for both boys and girls. Freed from the chador, women could take part in sports and other athletic activities. In 1939 scouting became compulsory for girls and boys. As Girl Guides, young women went hiking and camping. Fresh air, sunshine, and exercise strengthened girls' bodies.

Much of Iran's health-care system had been put into place by missionaries and Iranians who had studied medicine in Europe. Under Reza Shah, the government began adding state-run clinics and hospitals. Tehran's Hospital for Women, established in 1928, brought modern medicine to women. It also trained women to become nurses, midwives, and medical assistants. A school of midwifery opened in 1930. Iran was on track toward improving the health and longevity of women as well as opening career opportunities for them.

LEGAL REFORMS

Reza Shah's push for modernity included a reorganized Ministry of Justice. Just as the clergy feared, he created a whole new system of secular courts. The new legal codes were based on European models and replaced Islamic laws that treated men and women unequally as witnesses and victims. Family laws, however, remained much the same, although a few changes benefited women.

The marriage age for women was raised from nine to fifteen and for boys from fifteen to eighteen. Both bride and groom had to consent to the marriage. Young brides still needed their father's or grandfather's permission to marry. But once a woman was eighteen, if her father or guardian rejected her choice, she could petition the court for permission to marry a man she had chosen.

A new law required all marriages to be registered. A woman could now find out if her fiancé already had a wife (or wives). Women also won the right to specify "no second wife" in the marriage contract. A study of marriage contracts in Tehran in 1964 showed that 65 percent of women chose to do just that.

Polygamy, however, remained legal. So did temporary marriage—and honor killings. A man who killed his wife for committing adultery (having an affair) received no jail time. Men could still divorce a wife without giving a reason. She did not even have to be informed about it. Custody of children still went to the father or his male relatives after a divorce. The ex-wife could care for daughters to age seven and sons to age two "on behalf of the father"—provided she did not remarry during that time. Women still needed permission from their fathers or husbands to travel or work outside the home or to live apart from their families.

With his iron-fisted rule, Reza Shah kept the women's movement under his thumb. Educated upper-class women held low-level positions in the Ministry of Education, were principals of public and private schools, taught, and supervised the programs of the Ladies' Center. Women wore European-style hats and dresses and mixed socially with men. The nation's first coed elementary public school opened in 1935. The first woman professor at the University of Tehran, who had been educated in the Soviet Union, began teaching in 1942. These were visible changes, but in some ways Iranian women were less free. Under the shah's dictatorship, they could not organize, speak out, or demonstrate, much less vote or run for office.

CHAPTER 4

VICTORIES
FOR
WOMEN

"I ask you, how is it possible for a woman to perform the duties of motherhood . . . when her husband can divorce her at will and take away her children from her and leave their upbringing in someone else's hands?"

—Fatemeh Sayyah, university professor, working to influence the Majlis to reform family laws, 1944

When World War II (1939–1945) broke out in 1939, Iran declared itself neutral. But in the summer of 1941, Germany's army marched into the Soviet Union. The Allies (the nations fighting Germany) feared Reza Shah might join forces with German leader Adolf Hitler against them. In August 1941, two of the Allies, Britain and the Soviet Union, invaded Iran and forced Reza Shah to give up the throne. They sent the deposed shah into exile. His son, Mohammad Reza, was crowned shah in September, a month before his twenty-second birthday.

A TIME OF GREATER FREEDOM

The war years were difficult. British, Soviet, and U.S. troops occupied Iran and divided the nation into military sectors. Iran became a supply route for the Soviet Union. War materials and other goods traveled across the country from ports on the Persian Gulf north to the Caspian Sea. The country was also a haven for refugees from war-torn Eastern Europe. Wartime shortages of food and other necessities brought inflation, or rising prices.

But the chaos brought more freedom to Iranians. One freedom especially pleased women. With Reza Shah gone, police no longer enforced the unpopular unveiling law. Upper-class women and women of the middle class stuck to their fashionable hats. But most working-class women and the wives and daughters of bazaar merchants happily wrapped themselves once again in dark chadors. Few resumed wearing the face veil, however. It soon became a thing of the past. At last women had the right to dress as they wished.

Political parties came back to life. Besides liberals and conservatives, there were nationalists (who backed the constitution), royalists (who wanted a new monarchy), Communists and Socialists (who favored the elimination of private property), and Islamists (who advocated a government and a society based on the laws of Islam). All vied for seats in the Majlis.

Women, too, burst into the political arena. The Women's Association, part of the pro-Communist Tudeh Party, campaigned for equal pay and political rights for women. Its magazine, *Our Awakening*, trumpeted the slogan, "We, too, have rights in this country!"

A new Iranian Women's Party was formed. Fatemeh Sayyah, the first woman professor at Tehran University, took on the job of secretary. In 1944, when the Majlis debated voting laws, the Women's Party lobbied hard for woman suffrage. The issue met stiff resistance.

Many new, independent women's groups published periodicals.The teacher and writer Badr Bamdad founded the Iranian Women's League and edited its journal *Today's Woman*. Activist Dowlatabadi resumed publication of *Women's Voice*, this time as a magazine When she wrote an editorial asking the Allies to get out of Iran, however, the Allies closed the magazine down. Dozens of other women's groups issued magazines with assertive names: *Progressive Women, Women's Rights,The Emancipation of Women, Militant Women, Women's Revolt.*

The Allies won the war, and the Majlis once again debated giving women the vote. Both religious and secular deputies killed the bill. A cleric argued that it would bring "religious decay and social anarchy." A secular politician asserted, "Women do not have any psychological capacity for holding political status." If they become involved in politics, he claimed, "incredible chaos" will follow. "The natural duties of women, such as motherhood and other family tasks, will be either totally ignored or seen as insignificant."

RENEWED REPRESSION

In 1949 a popular leader, Mohammad Mosaddeq, united a number of parties within the Majlis to call for a return to the Constitution of 1906. But Mohammad Reza Shah wanted to rule Iran as his father had. He opposed giving up any political power to the Majlis.

The struggle between the shah and Mosaddeq came to a head over Iran's oil. In 1951 the Majlis approved a bill to nationalize, or take government control of, Iran's oil. The bill canceled all previous agreements allowing foreign companies to extract and sell Iran's oil. Britain, backed by the United States, objected. The shah did not want the agreements canceled, because he valued British and

U.S. support for his regime. The measure was so popular among Iranians, however, that the shah's rule was threatened. In 1953 the United States took the extreme measure of staging a coup, an overthrow of the government, using the Central Intelligence Agency (CIA), the agency authorized to carry out covert (secret) actions at the direction of the U.S. president to achieve U.S. policy objectives. By organizing riots, CIA agents overthrew Mosaddeq, who was tried and imprisoned. Mohammad Reza Shah, who had fled the unrest, returned to rule Iran.

Mohammad Reza Shah Pahlavi, shown here in 1965, first came to power during World War II in 1941, when British and Soviet troops forced his father to step down.

His authority restored, the shah cracked down on political parties. He banned the women's organizations of the pro-Communist and Socialist parties. Women's independent organizations and publications faced more censorship, and government agents kept a close watch over their activities.

In the same autocratic (dictatorial) fashion as his father, Mohammad Reza Shah began choosing which women's issues to back. Neither ruler cared much about women's rights, but both were concerned about Iran's image abroad. Having women lead active public lives was part of that image.

Mohammad Reza Shah also had two strong-minded women prodding him to do more for women. His twin sister, Ashraf, had knuckled under when her father forbade her to go to school in Switzerland and forced her to marry a man she did not like. She wanted to make sure that the next generation of Iranian girls would fare better. When Mohammad Reza Shah married Farah Diba, his third wife in 1959, his new queen added another voice urging him not to forget the women.

Social programs for poor women received the shah's support. In 1956 the Ministry of Labor founded the Welfare Council for Women and Children. Iran's first trained social worker, Sattareh Farman Farmaian, took on its leadership.

Princess Ashraf, Mohammad Reza Shah's twin sister, was a voice for Iranian women's rights within the shah's inner circle. She is shown here in 1940.

As a young woman, Farman Farmaian had badgered her father to allow her to study abroad as her brothers had done. He told her mother, "It would be a waste of money. She is a woman. A woman will be nothing." But in the end, he relented. She studied social work at the University of Southern California during World War II. She returned to Iran to improve orphanages and create centers for women and families in poor neighborhoods. She also founded Iran's first school of social work.

In 1961 women's groups joined forces to petition the shah for suffrage and other rights. In response, the shah created the High Council of Iranian Women. By appointing his sister Ashraf as president, he hoped to wield control over the women's movement. Many women's associations joined the council.

■ ■ ■ A HUGE LEAP

The shah announced a major reform program in 1963. He called it the White Revolution. Among other changes, it would give women the right to vote. Conservative clerics raised strong opposition to the program. The foremost objector was Ruhollah Mousavi Khomeini, a leading ayatollah, or expert in Shia Islam.

The shah scheduled a national vote for Iranians to accept or reject the reform program. The vote, on January 26, 1963, showed that a large majority favored the White Revolution. Women's groups marched to the imperial palace in celebration. "Our Revolution was not complete without women's full emancipation," the shah told them. "We have now made a huge leap from terrible backwardness into the ranks of civilized societies of the twentieth century."

That summer, Ayatollah Khomeini called for demonstrations against the White Revolution. The shah arrested Khomeini for his verbal attacks on the regime, provoking more demonstrations and rioting. The violence lasted three days, with many arrests, injuries, and deaths. The following year, after the ayatollah delivered more sermons denouncing the shah, Khomeini was sent into exile, first in Turkey and later in Iraq, where he remained until 1978.

AYATOLLAH

The title *ayatollah*, meaning "sign of God," is given to respected Islamic scholars. An ayatollah who is especially learned in the relationship of religion to social and political issues may become a *marja*, or "object of emulation." A marja is also known as a grand ayatollah. Shia Muslims consider grand ayatollahs supreme legal authorities. Ruhollah Mousavi Khomeini won recognition as a grand ayatollah in 1978.

Women, meanwhile, seized the opportunity to vote and run for office. In the September 1963 elections, six women won seats in the Majlis. The shah appointed two other women to the Senate. One of the newly elected deputies was Farrokhru Parsa, the daughter of the feminist leader Afaq Parsa.

Iranian women take part in demonstrations supporting a general election in Iran in August 1963. The women carried banners declaring support for the shah's reforms.

PROTECTING THE FAMILY

In 1965 members of the Association of Women Lawyers drafted proposals for major changes in the old Sharia-based family laws. The idea was not to kill Sharia. For every change under consideration, they consulted Islamic legal experts and won their support. The Ministry of Justice agreed to work with them the following year to write a bill to present to the Majlis. In 1967 their efforts paid off with the Family Protection Law.

Under this law, all marriage and divorce matters went to secular courts known as Family Protection Courts. No longer could a husband divorce his wife at will. He needed to gain the court's permission. Women won the right to sue for divorce for a variety of reasons. These included incompatibility and a husband taking a second wife against a first wife's wishes. Child custody was no longer automatically given to the father or his male relations, but rather was decided by the court.

Many opposed the new law. Ayatollah Khomeini was among those raising their voices against it. From his exile in Najaf, Iraq, he declared that the Family Protection Law "was passed in order to destroy the Muslim family. It is against Islam."

In 1975 women won more rights in the Family Protection Courts. The marriage age was once again raised, this time to eighteen for girls and twenty for boys. A number of issues remained unresolved, however. Women still could not travel outside Iran without the written consent of their husbands. Both the absence of punishment for honor killings and the unequal inheritance laws stayed as they were. Polygamy and temporary marriage remained legal. But progress had been made. Women knew they had to choose their battles carefully to avoid a backlash from conservative clerics and traditionalists.

NEW HORIZONS FOR WOMEN

During this time, the government expanded the number of girls' schools and coeducational schools. By the late 1970s, women made up 38 percent of the elementary school population in Iran.

More women were also heading to college. Tehran University was no longer the only university in Iran. The shah had ordered new universities in other cities. He modeled them on universities in the United States. Professors came from the United States to teach classes and help organize the new schools.

Both men and women attended these universities. Shirin Ebadi, who studied law at the University of Tehran in the 1960s, noted that almost all of her women classmates wore Western fashions. Only three wore veils. The rest dressed in miniskirts and teased their hair into bouffant styles, just like U.S. coeds. Unlike in U.S. college life, however, the young men and women did not mix much. Women sat in the front of the class, men at the back. Nobody dated.

Besides the coeducational colleges, a women's college, the Higher Educational Institute for Girls, was founded in 1964 in northern Tehran. (Later it was renamed the Farah Pahlavi University in honor of Iran's queen.)

As more upper-class Iranians began allowing their daughters to study abroad, Europe and the United States gave Iranian women additional options for higher education. One of these daughters, Farah Diba, was studying architecture in France when the shah chose her as his third wife. By 1979 about eighty thousand Iranians were enrolled in foreign universities. A sizable minority of them were women.

Traditional views of women still held sway outside of major urban centers. Even so, a few women from villages and towns succeeded in getting their parents' permission to go on their own to universities in Iran's larger cities.

Employment opportunities opened up as well. Large numbers of women worked in government offices. For the first time, women served on the police force. In 1968 Farrokhru Parsa, who was among the first women Majlis deputies, became Iran's first woman cabinet member when she was appointed minister of education. Other women became deputy (assistant) ministers. The first women judges, a group of five, were appointed the following year. In 1970 Shirin Ebadi became a judge at the age of twenty-three.

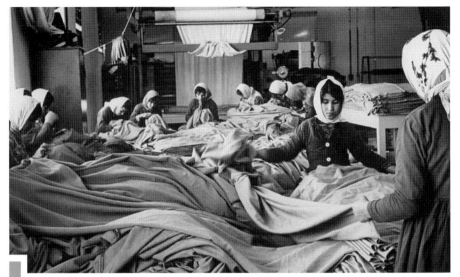

Above: Women work in a textile factory in Iran in 1965. As Iranian women were granted more freedom, the number of women working in factories and other businesses increased as well. *Below*: Iran's Queen Farah Diba is crowned empress at ceremonies in 1967. She is the only woman in Iran's history to be named empress.

It wasn't just the government offering jobs. Private companies hired women too. Women worked in factories and as secretaries. Some reached management positions in business.

Men still remained at the top of most organizations, but it seemed only a matter of time before women would become executives and leaders, and maybe even rulers. In 1967 the shah determined that if he died before his son, the Crown Prince Reza, was old enough to rule, his capable wife Queen Farah should reign until the boy reached the age of twenty.

MOVING TOWARD GENDER EQUALITY

In 1966 the High Council of Women's Organizations of Iran became the Women's Organization of Iran (WOI) under the leadership of Princess Ashraf. Fifty-one women's organizations joined the WOI and worked together toward gender equality. Part of their effort was directed to lobbying the Majlis for additions to the Family Protection Law and more laws to help working mothers.

Even more effort was devoted to winning over poor and working-class women. Burdened by poverty, these women had little time to give to women's rights. To reach them, WOI expanded its network of services. In centers and branches across the country, staffed by professionals and an army of volunteers, the WOI ran literacy classes, helped women find jobs, gave free legal advice, and provided day care for children. Lectures, radio talks, and pamphlets taught women their legal rights, helped women gain confidence in their capabilities, and raised their expectations.

> "It is great if I am aware of my individual rights and of the law the parliament has passed to preserve those rights. But of what use is the awareness or the law if I do not know how I will provide my child with the needed daily bread, or shelter, or clothing?"
>
> —Mahnaz Afkhami, quoting the response of poor Iranian women to the Iranian women's movement in the late 1960s

During the 1970s, the WOI grew to 118 centers with four hundred branches. An estimated one million poor and working-class women used and benefited from their services each year.

In 1976 the secretary general of the WOI, Mahnaz Afkhami, was named Iran's first minister of state for women's affairs. She initiated a survey of Iranian women to find out how to improve women's status.

After two years of conducting about seven hundred seminars in every province, the WOI prepared its report, the National Plan of Action. It gave the government a "road map to gender equality." The cabinet endorsed it in 1978.

By 1979 the progress of women in Iran had been remarkable. Two million Iranian women had joined the workforce. The 1976-1977 census listed women as 53 percent of Iran's teachers and 48 percent of its medical students. Women also worked in the army and police force, and as lawyers, judges, pilots, engineers, university professors, businesswomen, and civil servants (government employees). In 1978, women made up 37 percent of all university students.

More than three hundred women served on local government councils, twenty-two held seats in the Majlis, five were mayors of cities, and three held high positions in government ministries. One was a cabinet minister, one a governor, and one an ambassador.

GROWING OPPOSITION TO THE SHAH

Women's gains came at a cost. To advance their goals, women activists had allied themselves with an increasingly autocratic ruler. Mohammad Reza Shah had silenced Mosaddeq with help from the United States in 1953. But the followers of the popular politician remained angry. They wanted a parliamentary government, not a dictator.

The shah had exiled Ayatollah Khomeini, but he could not silence him. From Najaf, Khomeini raged against the shah in sermons on Friday, Islam's holy day. Audiotapes of his sermons, smuggled into Iran, circulated throughout the country. Many clergy and pious citizens agreed with his criticism.

The two principal anti-shah factions differed widely. One wanted a secular, modern Iran. The other wanted an Islamic republic guided by religious principles and traditional values.

One issue that united the shah's opponents was the growing gap between rich and poor. Iran's oil wealth had brought an economic boom. But the money enriched the royal family, military officers, and businesses connected to the shah. Foreign businesses bringing technological expertise also profited. The streets, restaurants, hotels, and nightclubs of Tehran filled with rich Americans and Europeans. In northern Tehran, large palaces and villas with elegant gardens housed the wealthy. The poor struggled in shantytowns (slums) in the southern part of the city. And for all the charitable work of the women's groups, Iran had one of the worst infant mortality (death) rates in the Middle East. For all the new universities, 68 percent of adults could not read and 60 percent of children did not finish elementary school.

A second issue was repression. Since the 1950s, political parties, labor unions, and newspapers had faced increasing curbs on their activities. A key enforcement arm of the shah's policies was SAVAK, the Persian acronym for Organization for National Security and Information. Established in 1957, SAVAK assigned agents to keep tabs on citizens suspected of being involved in anti-shah political activities. At times SAVAK imprisoned and tortured innocent people. In 1975 the human rights organization Amnesty International pronounced Iran "one of the world's worst violators of human rights."

■ THE SHAH FALLS

In the mid-1970s, when inflation struck economies worldwide, the number of Iranians dissatisfied with the shah soared. Demands for change erupted everywhere: Abolish one-party rule. Dismantle SAVAK. Let the Ayatollah Khomeini return to Iran. What began as angry letters turned into angry marches, mobs, strikes, and riots. Violent clashes between police and civilians brought arrests, injuries, deaths, and more outrage. Unrest continued throughout 1978.

Women found themselves on both sides of the revolt. Many feminists wanted reform, but supported the shah out of gratitude for all he had done for women. But others marched in the protests, wearing chadors to show their solidarity with women from traditional backgrounds. They did not imagine that a regime change would deprive them of their rights.

The shah's efforts to appease the rioters had already taken the women's movement a step backward. In the summer of 1978, he

Above: Iranian women participate in anti-shah demonstrations on the streets of Tehran in 1978. *Below*: Iranian women show their support for the shah by carrying a photo of the shah and his family in 1978.

abolished the Ministry of Women's Affairs. His rapidly changing prime ministers (four in 1978) appointed no women at all in their cabinets.

That November, the former minister of women's affairs, Mahnaz Afkhami, was at the United Nations (UN), an international organization promoting cooperation among governments, in New York City. She was there to discuss plans for a research institute in Tehran for the advancement of women. She received a call warning her not to return to Iran. Knowing that, as a leading feminist, she would be a target if Islamic conservatives gained power, she resigned from the WOI and applied for asylum (political refuge) in the United States. She was one of the few to foresee that the era of advancing women's rights in Iran was about to end.

CHAPTER 5

A GIANT LEAP
BACKWARD

I don't know that I want. . . .
Freedom is so new here. I only
know I don't want to go back to
chador. I don't want to exchange
one dictatorship with another."

—Thirty-year-old woman psychologist in Tehran, March 1979

In January 1979, the shah assigned a special council to run the country, and he departed Iran. It made sense to escape while he could, as nothing he could do would save his regime. Although he did not reveal it publicly at the time, he was also ill with cancer. On February 1, Ayatollah Khomeini landed in Tehran. More than 3 million Iranians lined the streets leading from the airport into the city to welcome him.

Ten days later, revolutionary forces overcame the last resistance from the Iranian army and the Imperial Guard, the shah's 18,000 elite troops. Ayatollah Khomeini set up the Revolutionary Council to restore order. The council appointed a new prime minister, Mehdi Bazargan, to lead a provisional (temporary) government. Neither the Revolutionary Council nor Bazargan's provisional government included any women.

In spite of the lack of women in the new, temporary governing bodies, many women did not believe that their lives would change. That confidence was soon shaken.

One early sign of a new trend was the declaration on February 26 that the Family Protection Laws of 1967 and 1975 were suspended. All the changes in marriage, divorce, and custody laws that women had fought for in the 1960s and 1970s were lost. Girls could be married at age nine, husbands could divorce their wives at will. Days later, the Ministry

Ayatollah Khomeini greets crowds of supporters in Tehran in February 1979. Khomeini had just returned from fifteen years in exile.

of Justice declared it would appoint no new women judges. Women lawyers who qualified for assignment as judges, the minister said, were welcome to apply for office jobs in the ministry. After their years of legal training, these women could be only secretaries or law clerks. The minister of defense added a third rebuff to women on March 6. All army corpswomen were dismissed. No women would be allowed to serve in the army in the future.

■ ■ ■ AT THE DAWN OF FREEDOM, WE HAVE NO FREEDOM

On March 7 Ayatollah Khomeini, speaking to students of theology in Qom, dropped another bombshell on women's rights. "Now that we have in Iran an Islamic government," he said, "women should observe Islamic criteria of dress, particularly those that work in the ministries."

The following day, March 8, was International Women's Day. To celebrate, a group of women activists had planned a memorial for women who had lost their lives in the revolution. But after Khomeini's speech, alarmed women telephoned friends and colleagues. The scheduled memorial shifted to a protest against what was happening to the living. The numbers planning to attend swelled. Even warnings of a late-winter snowstorm did not put anyone off.

Farzaeh Nouri, a lawyer, said, "I'll never wear a veil. I'll never wear a chador. I'll never put on a scarf. No man—not the Shah, not Khomeini, and not anyone else—will ever make me dress as he pleases. The women of Iran have been unveiled for three generations, and we will fight anyone who bars our way,"

Her angry words fired up the women gathered at Tehran University's faculty of fine arts. The audience, most of them dressed in skirts or jeans, responded with chants of "Death to despotism [a government with absolute power] under any cover!" The hall was jammed. Outside in the snow, two thousand more women and a few hundred men listened to Nouri's amplified speech.

The protesters included women from many different fields. Women working for the Iranian airline released a statement declaring that the only veil women need is "a veil of purity which is in their hearts." Nurses in government hospitals, teachers in high schools, and women employees of the Ministries of Agriculture and Foreign Affairs joined the demonstration.

The protest was not about veiling. The real issue was freedom. And freedom of dress was only one of several items on the agenda. Speeches and slogans also demanded equal wages, more say in government, and a reinstatement of the Family Protection Laws. "We condemn all forms of repression," the protesters cried. "We shall not let anyone turn us into slaves in the name of democracy."

In a spontaneous move, the protesters decided to take their demands to the offices of Prime Minister Bazargan. Crowds gathered along the route to watch the thousands of marchers. As they passed schools, girls cheered them from classroom windows. Clusters of women left shops and offices to join the parade. Angry men began to taunt the women, calling them prostitutes and foreign agents. Soon the hecklers were pelting the women with snowballs and spit. "Wear a head wrap or get a head rap!" they yelled.

Revolutionary forces in charge of keeping order stood by, watching, doing nothing to prevent the abuse. The women pressed closer together and kept marching. The demonstration swelled to an estimated ten thousand protesters. Before the stream of marchers reached their goal, the revolutionaries moved in. Shooting rifles and machine guns into the air, the guards broke up the protest and the swarms of hecklers. The women disbanded, grateful to escape the roiling mob.

Their protest was not over. It resumed the next day, and the next, and for two more days after that. Over five days, in a dozen or more demonstrations, women made their voices heard. Both veiled and unveiled women walked off their jobs or out of their classrooms to join the protesters. They gathered in front of the national radio and television offices to condemn the lack of media coverage of their demonstrations. A crowd of fifteen thousand staged a sit-in at the Ministry of Justice to protest its refusal to appoint new women judges.

Women fill the streets of Tehran in a protest for equal rights on March 12, 1979.

Thousands filled the gymnasium at Tehran University to hear speeches from politicians who supported women's rights. They defied the attacks of conservative opponents. The air of Tehran rang with feminist slogans. "We want equal rights," they shouted. "At the dawn of freedom, we have no freedom." According to a United Nations report prepared in 2009, these spontaneous demonstrations were "the largest in the history of women's movements in Iran."

A SMALL VICTORY—FOR THE TIME BEING

The government tried to calm the storm with reassurances. The deputy prime minister announced that women government employees would not be required to wear the traditional chador but should "dress with dignity and avoid appearing cheap or exposed in their offices." He condemned the attacks on the women marchers. The public prosecutor promised to arrest anyone caught attacking unveiled women.

> "I will wear a chador on the day all Iranian men start wearing turbans and stop shaving their faces, as Islam law says they must."
>
> —Female government secretary speaking to a colleague, March 8, 1979

Ayatollah Taleqani, the religious leader of Tehran, issued a statement on civil liberties. In it he offered the opinion that hijab was not an obligation in Islam. Rather, it was a duty to be taken up voluntarily.

The women retreated. They had at least won the point that they could dress as they wished.

But as a woman professor of economics pointed out, the numbers who turned out to protest "form a speck of the population. That's all. Just a speck." In all, there were probably two hundred thousand similarly minded women in Iran, she estimated. That was less than 2 percent of the female adult population.

In 1979 the vast majority of Iranian women were not worried about gender equality. They were more worried about food and shelter. One peasant woman, the mother of six children, felt she had equality enough. "Everyone in my family is equal to everyone else in my family," she said. "My husband of twenty-five years and my children and myself can afford meat only once every two months. We eat the same thing and we work the same. I ask you, where is this not balanced?"

Most men, even liberal ones, also saw women's issues as less important. "The question of women is not the main one," said a leader of the Mojahedin-e Khalq party, a radical Islamist group with many women members. More important, he said, "is the need to sweep away the traces of imperialism [the shah's foreign-supported autocratic regime]." Another man, who held secular, pro-democratic political views, saw the protests as merely a question of clothing. "So what?" he commented. "It won't kill women to wear scarves for a while."

The educated, Westernized women who took part in the protests did not want to push things too far. Feeling that the government had yielded to their pressure, many believed it was a time for calm. "We made our point and received the answer we sought," a woman architect explained. "But then it began to look like the women were against the Imam [a title of honor in Shia Islam given to Khomeini]. Now is not the time for a split here."

TWO REFERENDA CREATE THE ISLAMIC REPUBLIC OF IRAN

The various factions that supported the revolution now had to form a government. In this, Khomeini had the advantage over the politicians. United only by their opposition to the shah, the political parties held a variety of views. They lacked strong leadership, experience in government, and sources of income. Khomeini was a well-known and popular leader, with wealthy Shia institutions to back him and a network of mosques throughout the country to depend on. In neighborhoods and towns, local clergy had already formed komitehs (committees) to police the streets and support Khomeini. The komitehs recruited young men loyal to Khomeini into militias (local military groups). These militias later formed the core of the Revolutionary Guard, a branch of Iran's military.

Khomeini scheduled a referendum for April 1. The ballot read: "Islamic Republic—Yes or No?" Politicians requested the addition of the word democratic, but Khomeini rejected the term as too Western. He told an interviewer later, "Islam does not need adjectives such as democratic."

The people agreed. Out of an electorate of twenty-one million, twenty million turned out to vote. Of those, 99 percent of them voted yes.

In August, elections were held for seventy-three delegates to form an assembly to draft an Islamic constitution for Iran. Committees appointed by Khomeini screened all candidates for the election. The majority of those elected were high-ranking clergy. Only one was a woman.

Monireh Gorji, the sole woman, had taught Arabic and the Quran before the revolution. She attended the sessions wrapped in a chador, but she was not afraid to speak up. Deftly citing the Quran, she defended women's equality as an Islamic principle. She argued for more education for women and for fairer family laws. But she was not powerful enough to challenge the male delegates when they barred women from serving as judges or as a supreme leader.

The secular politicians were not happy with the constitution the assembly drafted. It undermined the principle of representative government, they argued, and raised the clergy into a "ruling class." Prime Minister Bazargan threatened to publish his own draft constitution and put it to a vote against Khomeini's. But other circumstances intervened.

In late October 1979, U.S. president Jimmy Carter agreed to allow the exiled shah to enter the United States for cancer treatment. On November 4, about four hundred university students, armed with bolt cutters, clubs, and a few guns, snipped open gates and climbed 8-foot (2.5 meter) walls to seize the U.S. Embassy in Tehran. They were angry with the United States for helping the shah.

Iranian students stand guard in front of the U.S. Embassy in Tehran in November 1979. The students took over the embassy to protest the U.S. decision to allow the exiled shah to enter the United States for medical treatment. A portrait of Ayatollah Khomeini hangs above them.

They took employees hostage and demanded that the United States hand the shah over to Iran for trial. When Khomeini refused to stop the students, Bazargan resigned as prime minister. The students' sit-in and hostage holding, planned to last a few days, stretched into 444 days.

Taking advantage of the crisis, Khomeini scheduled a referendum on the constitution for December 2. He warned voters that the United States was poised to invade Iran at the first sign of disunity. This time only sixteen million went to the polls, but again 99 percent voted for the Constitution of the Islamic Republic of Iran. Their vote legitimized Khomeini as the ruler of Iran.

One young woman active in the Iranian Revolution became a national hero. Massoumeh Ebtekar was nineteen years old when she took part in the student invasion of the U.S. Embassy in Tehran. The daughter of an engineer who had earned his PhD at the University of Pennsylvania, Ebtekar attended elementary school in Philadelphia, Pennsylvania. Because she spoke fluent English, she became the spokesperson of the group, which called itself Students Following the Imam's Line.

She was also well-versed in revolutionary speech. "She talked my ear off about the revolution, about the ayatollah, about politics, about the shah, and about SAVAK, the shah's secret police—she went on and on," said a U.S. marine security guard, one of the hostages held for 444 days.

After the hostages were released, the student leaders of the occupation were rewarded with political appointments. Twenty-one-year-old Ebtekar was made editor of the English-language edition of *Kayhan*, a government-sponsored newspaper.

Massoumeh Ebtekar, one of the students who invaded the U.S. Embassy in Tehran in 1979, is shown here in 2007.

Iran's Constitution of 1979, still in force in 2011, is based almost entirely on principles Khomeini called "the guardianship of the jurist [legal expert]," a system of religious rule he devised while in exile. It included elements from European constitutions, as requested by the prime minister. In this hybrid document, the people elect a president, a legislature (the Majlis), and an Assembly of Experts. The Assembly of Experts, made up of clerics, chooses a prominent male religious figure to be Supreme Leader.

The Supreme Leader holds office for life or until the Assembly of Experts deems him incapable of fulfilling his duties. He wields wide-ranging authority. He appoints the chief judge, the commanders of the armed forces, and six members of a powerful body called the Guardian Council. He approves candidates for office, declares war and peace, sets guidelines for the republic, and appoints the high officials of a wide range of government-run institutions, such as the national radio and television network and Iran's two leading newspapers. He can also dismiss presidents. He has far more power than Mohammad Reza Pahlavi ever did as shah.

The Guardian Council is made up of six religious scholars appointed by the Supreme Leader and six legal experts selected by the chief judge and approved by the Majlis. This council may veto (turn down) any bills passed by the Majlis that it judges to be unconstitutional or un-Islamic. An additional body called the Expediency Council was added later to mediate conflicts between the Majlis and the Guardian Council. This council is appointed by the Supreme Leader.

■ ■ ■ WOMEN GO THEIR SEPARATE WAYS

The women's movement that erupted so suddenly in March died away. A few hardy souls did their best to keep the struggle alive. The women whose nominations for judges had been thrown out attended the ceremony installing the new male judges into office. They demonstrated for five days but achieved no results. Women employees of a government corporation held a demonstration when their day-care center was closed. It remained closed. The company threatened to lay off employees who did not return to work.

Meanwhile, the losses for women mounted. At the end of March Khomeini announced that beaches and sports events would be segregated (separated) by gender. In May the Ministry of Education banned coeducation. Schools or departments with too few women students to justify the expense of separate classes refused to register women. Especially hard hit were women students in engineering, science, and other technical courses. They were told to change their majors to fields with more women students. A month later, the same ministry banned married women from high schools.

That summer, the government segregated beaches along the Caspian Sea into men's and women's sections. Komiteh officers patrolled the

This sign on an Iranian beach on the Caspian Sea tells people that the beach is separated into men's and women's sections.

beach and whipped women caught swimming in the men's area. The humiliating public punishment was new to Iran. The same harsh penal code (laws concerning punishment) also led to the deaths by execution of three women accused of prostitution.

In October the Revolutionary Council passed new family legislation. It set the marriage age for girls at thirteen. Since the ministry of education blocked married women from attending school, that meant many young women would not go to middle or high school. The right of divorce returned to the husband, who no longer had to seek permission from the court. The law also reinstated the husband's right to forbid his wife to work and, if divorced, his right to custody of his children.

■ PINK SLIPS AND WORSE

Days after the new family laws passed, Shirin Ebadi received notice that she was dismissed from her judgeship and demoted to law clerk. "Show up to the legal office," the the man in charge of dismissals told her as he shoved a paper across the table to where she stood.

Ebadi was distressed at being dismissed after ten successful years as a judge. She followed the instructions, however, and showed up punctually at the legal office where judiciary clerks came to get their assignments. Once there, she announced that since she had been demoted against her will, she would do no work in protest. She sat there day after day for weeks and weeks, protesting, until the birth of her first child freed her for a two-month maternity leave. Ebadi later returned to work as secretary of the court where she had once presided as judge.

Dismissals were common. Almost all of the women who had risen to positions of importance during the monarchy lost their jobs. Among them were 22 Majlis deputies, 330 women serving on local government councils, 5 mayors, and thousands of civil servants.

For some women, exile was preferable to living in the Islamic Republic of Iran. But getting a visa to leave the country was not easy. After seeing her college of social work taken over by revolutionary students who accused her of supporting the shah, Sattareh Farman Farmaian feared for her life if she remained in Iran. She managed to get an exit visa and found Tehran's airport overflowing with refugees hoping to catch flights out of the country. She was relieved to snag a seat on a plane to Pakistan.

Those without visas paid bandits to smuggle them across deserts and mountains to Turkey or Pakistan, an expensive and harrowing experience. But for anyone linked to the shah's administration, it was worth it. Remaining in Iran was dangerous. Groups of revolutionaries took the law into their own hands. Revolutionary courts held speedy trials that allowed no defense or appeal. Farrokhru Parsa, who had served as minister of education under the shah, was brought before such a tribunal (court). The court charged her with promoting prostitution and ordered her immediate execution. Placed in a bag, she was brutally machine-gunned to death.

As the tumultuous year drew to an end, women activists held a conference to discuss how to proceed. By gathering various women's organizations together, they hoped to create an effective umbrella organization to coordinate their efforts. Aware of the opposition to such an organization, they avoided publicizing their meeting. But word leaked out. To stop the conference from taking place, the revolutionary government cut off electricity to the building where the women planned to meet. The Conference of the Unity of Women met anyway—by candlelight.

The candlelight, the cold, and the dark December day suited the mood of the meeting. Not only had women lost ground, they had also splintered into factions. Differing political views pulled women apart. Most of the remaining women's groups were the women's branches of various political parties. Their loyalty was to their party, not to the women's movement. The close cooperation needed for a strong women's movement was not possible. It looked like Iranian women, a year earlier among the most liberated in the Muslim Middle East, would once again be chained to the dictates of a conservative religious patriarchy.

CHAPTER 6

THE DAWN OF MUSLIM WOMEN

"Today they've told me to wear a scarf. Tomorrow I'll be told not to go back to work . . . and the day after tomorrow, they'll tell us we can't drive a car and we can only stay in the house."

—Bookstore owner in Tehran, July 5, 1980

Over the winter and spring of 1980, it became clear that the victory women won the previous March was not going to last. In February the minister of health ordered nurses and all women working at his ministry, including non-Muslims, to wear uniforms that complied with the conservative Islamic standards. Then the Ministry of Justice required women employees to wear "simple and Islamic clothes." By late June, Ayatollah Khomeini declared an "administrative revolution." All women working for the government were to wear Islamic hijab, he announced. Many women civil servants resumed wearing chadors, but soon more practical Islamic attire became popular. Hoods, robes, tunics, and wide trousers could cover the women as well as a chador and freed their hands for work.

In early July, in a last desperate attempt to defend their freedom of dress, women staged a demonstration. About twenty-five hundred women turned out, most dressed in black as though for a funeral.

Women gather outside the office of Iran's new president, Abolhassan Banisadr, in Tehran in July 1980. The women were demonstrating for freedom of dress.

Abolhassan Banisadr was elected the first president of Iran in February 1980. But Supreme Leader Khomeini held more political power.

They gathered in front of the office of the recently elected first president of Iran, Abolhassan Banisadr. "We didn't have a revolution to march backward," they chanted.

The president may well have sympathized with the women. But any attempt to overrule the Supreme Leader would have cost him his position. Many feminists stayed out of the protest for similar reasons. "There is no way to fight it, and we have more important issues to discuss," said one activist.

Angry conservatives—men and women both—staged a counterprotest. "Death to the foreign dolls," they chanted. The protesters called themselves Hezbollahis, that is, members of Hezbollah, the "Party of God." The name meant that in their eyes they were not acting for any political party or following any political leader. Their leader was God.

The women's demonstration was doomed from the start. Already large numbers of Iranian women were wearing some form of veiling that covered hair, torsos, arms, and legs, leaving only their hands and faces bare. For many the motive was religious. For others it was fear of harassment. Religious fanatics had attacked women in small towns for going out bareheaded. Some women had been stabbed with knives. Many merchants would not permit unveiled women to enter their shops. In one town, merchants who sold goods to unveiled women found their shops threatened with closure.

Over the summer, veiling rules increased. During the holy month of Ramadan all women were ordered to don hijab in public. The street campaign against women who did not comply with the dress code grew more vicious. Gangs of lawless groups took even stronger measures than the komiteh patrols. One August evening in Tehran, a group of men stopped a car with a married couple inside. Discovering that the woman was wearing a sleeveless dress, the men declared she must be punished. They gave her a choice. Did she want her right arm slashed with a knife or splashed with acid? The terrified woman opted for the knife. Afterward, it took dozens of stitches to close the gash.

It was hardly an isolated case. Every day, in towns and cities throughout the country, anonymous assailants attacked women with stones, clubs, knives, razors, or chemicals for minor infractions— lipstick, nail polish, wisps of hair showing, bare feet in sandals. Khomeini spoke out against the violence, but police did not arrest the vigilantes.

A conservative Islamist man carries his daughter, covered in a black chador, while talking to another man on the street in Tehran in 1980. His wife follows behind, also wearing a chador and veil covering her face. Women did not have to be completely covered when out on the streets, but faced harassment and violence if they did not don hijab in public.

A female office worker wears the Islamic hijab while riding an elevator in Tehran in 1980. All women in Iran were ordered by the government to wear hijab earlier that year.

The veil had become an icon of the revolution in Iran. It marked Iran as Islamic. As Ayatollah Taleqani noted, "We want to show that there has been a revolution, a profound change." In celebration of this icon, for the first time in Iran's history, the government issued a postage stamp with a woman on it. It featured a woman's face surrounded by a black hood.

"I do not like to wear the Islamic hijab. . . . But now that I am covered head to toe at work my expertise is appreciated much more than under the previous system. Now they [my male colleagues] look at me as a scientist while before they looked at me as a sex object."

—*Zohreh, a woman manager of a chemical laboratory, Tehran, 1989*

A stark example of the anger the Islamists felt toward unveiled women occurred in August 1980. Sediqeh Dowlatabadi, a feminist leader from the 1920s to the 1950s, was one of the first Iranian women who dared to go unveiled on the streets of Tehran. All her life, she had been strongly opposed to the veil, which she saw as a symbol of women's subjection to men. Before she died in 1961, she wrote, "I will never forgive women who visit my grave veiled." In 1980 Islamists destroyed the memorial over her grave.

MOTHERHOOD AND FAMILY

Iranian women naturally worried about what would come next. The new constitution guaranteed women and men equal protection under the law. But that was qualified by the phrase "in conformity with Islamic criteria." It also assured the rights of women, again "in conformity with Islamic criteria." Sharia-based legislation would replace the Westernized legal codes that Reza Shah had instituted. In stating the nation's goals for women, the constitution stressed motherhood, family, and child-rearing.

Women had already been deprived of judgeships. The constitution made clear that women could not aspire to Supreme Leadership of the country. At universities and colleges, gender segregation was closing women out of many science and technology courses. Women lawyers, engineers, and professors also lost jobs. Women nurses were dismissed for not wearing Islamic outfits. Women teachers were fired for speaking to male colleagues. Women assembly-line workers were replaced with men. Economic problems caused by the revolution hurt many businesses, adding to the excuses for letting women go.

Before the revolution, Khomeini reassured women that they would remain in the workforce. "As for women," he said, "Islam has never been against their freedom. . . . A woman is man's equal; she and he are both free to choose their lives and their occupations." In speeches after the revolution, he urged women to help build the new nation. "Just as you had a fundamental role in the movement," he told a group of women, "you must also have a share in the victory."

Yet a book he published soon after his return to Iran in 1979 shocked women with its conservative views. A typical statement declared, "A married woman should not leave the house without permission of her husband."

The government also used indirect means to discourage women from working. It closed day-care centers. Women who asked for a day off to care for a sick child were advised to quit work.

Meanwhile, Khomeini held up motherhood as the primary role of women. Government policy encouraged women to have children. Abortion, sterilization, and birth control were made illegal. New family laws allowed husbands to forbid their wives to work outside the home. Fatima, a daughter of the prophet Muhammad, became the model of Islamic womanhood for Iranian women. As the wife of Ali, the founder of Shia Islam, and the mother of two Shia imams, she holds a special place in Shia faith. In May 1979 Khomeini declared Fatima's birthday as the new Women's Day, to replace the March 8 International Women's Day in Iran.

Muslim feminist author Zahra Rahnavard joined the chorus praising family life. In a book entitled *The Dawn of Muslim Woman*, she declared, "Motherhood and wifehood is the road to freedom and liberation."

WAR PROVIDES WORK FOR WOMEN

In 1980 President Saddam Hussein of Iraq ordered an invasion of Iran. Iraq was trying to gain control of Shatt al Arab, the river between the two countries that gives Iraq access to the Persian Gulf. The war that followed lasted eight years. So many men were drafted to defend Iran, and later to attack Iraq, that women were needed to keep the country functioning.

Women took on civil service jobs. They worked in army laundries, kitchens, and hospitals. Good day-care centers became a necessity so that mothers could serve the nation at war, and the government began to provide them. In 1984 Khomeini ruled that "Women can participate in economic, political and social affairs within the Islamic laws and regulations." The war had changed the roles of Iranian women. The following year, Khomeini even allowed women to serve in the military, a complete about-face from his earlier ruling.

The numbers of working women, which had declined after the revolution, picked up. By the mid-1980s the percentage

Female members of the Iranian military march in a rally in Tehran in 1988. For practical reasons, Ayatollah Khomeini allowed women to serve in the nation's military during the war with Iraq.

of women employed in government ministries was the same as it had been in the mid-1970s.

The gender separation policy of the Islamic government in some cases added more women to the workforce. On factory assembly lines, women supervisors were needed to oversee women workers. Hair salons and clothing stores catering to women could hire only women employees. Women with cars started "lady cabs" for women, since they were not allowed to ride in cars with men unrelated to them.

Gender segregation also made employment outside the home more appealing to religious women. They did not have to fear the "moral decay" that clergy said resulted from working alongside men.

Enterprising women started their own informal businesses. They sold crafts, food, and plants that they made or grew themselves. Since they were self-employed, they could adjust their work schedules around their household and child-raising duties.

Allowing women to work did not change government policy on veiling or its view of women's place in society. Just the opposite happened. The increased contact between men and women at work required stricter enforcement of the moral codes. Leaders also emphasized that women's jobs must not interfere with their roles as wives and mothers.

Men remained the bosses and decision-makers in both public and private concerns. In every workplace, women's progress lagged far behind men's. Nationwide, the census figures for 1986 show that the percentage of women employed was only 7.3 percent of the female population age 10 and over. That was down from 10.2 percent in 1976. Male employment, however, had increased from 89.8 percent in 1976 to 92.7 percent in 1986. The job gap between men and women had widened significantly.

The kinds of jobs open to women also blocked women's progress. Highly educated women, especially in technical fields such as architecture and engineering, often had to settle for low-level jobs in schools and day-care centers. Many businesses and government agencies gave men priority over women in hiring or simply refused to hire women at all.

WOMEN IN POLITICS AND PUBLIC LIFE

Ayatollah Khomeini had strongly opposed women's voting in 1963, but by 1979 he saw the matter with new eyes. Women were among his strongest supporters. Their votes on the referenda had helped establish the Islamic Republic. He was no longer willing to deny women the vote or the chance to hold public office.

In June 1980, elections for the first Islamic Majlis took place. Under the rules of the new constitution, all candidates were screened by Khomeini and the Assembly of Experts. Of the 270 deputies elected, four were women. (In the last Majlis before the revolution, twenty-two women had been deputies.) All were devout women who belonged to the Islamic Republican Party. The number of women deputies did not rise in the 1980s. It remained four in 1984 and fell to three in 1988.

The women deputies did their best to broaden women's rights. They faced tough opposition from hard-line clerics in the Majlis but managed to win a few victories. One new law allowed women civil servants to work part-time for a proportion of the full-time salary based on the number of hours worked instead of much lower hourly wages. Another law gave women widowed by the war with Iraq custody of their children. (Sharia law gave custody to a child's paternal grandfather or other male member of the deceased father's family.) The women deputies also created a Majlis committee focused on women, youth, and family issues. These advances were small but significant, as they set the stage for future legislation.

Women deputies in the third Majlis (1988–1992) pushed the envelope a bit further. A new law set up special courts to hear family disputes. These courts ruled on divorce. Under this law, a husband could not legally divorce a wife without a good reason that conformed to Sharia law. Women served as special advisers in these courts. Shirin Ebadi was among the women chosen to fill this position. Another law provided divorced women with a cash settlement based on the number of years they had worked as housewives and mothers.

Steps such as these slowly added to women's legal rights. They also gave women hope that political action could bring about a more liberal and democratic, yet still Islamic republic.

Above: Women's rights activist Shirin Ebadi was chosen as an adviser to Iran's family courts after having been removed as a judge years earlier.
Right: Zahra Rahnavard was one of the founders of the Women's Society of Islamic Revolution in the 1980s.

WOMEN'S ORGANIZATIONS AND PUBLICATIONS

During the revolution, many women's organizations had sprouted, most of them linked to revolutionary political parties. By 1981 the government had banned most of these parties, leaving their women's branches stranded. But women who supported Islamic rule formed new organizations. Like the Majlis deputies, they worked within the regime's ideology.

One of the most influential groups was the Women's Society of Islamic Revolution (WSIR), formed soon after the revolution. Its founders included women who had studied at universities in the United States. Once they had adopted Western ways, but they had changed their views during the revolution. Their goal was to create a new identity for Iranian women that was at once Islamic and Persian—not secular or Western.

One founder of WSIR was Zahra Rahnavard. She advocated replacing traditional Islam, which had been influenced by centuries of male interpreters using the religion to reinforce patriarchy. Instead she suggested a "true Islam" as preached and lived by the prophet Muhammed.

WSIR leaders arranged seminars with the clerics in charge of the courts to discuss women's problems with the legal system. Branches of the WSIR opened in provincial towns to raise women's awareness of their rights within Islam. The government, however, soon sidelined the women who founded the organization. It replaced the leadership with more conservative women who did not question the traditional patriarchal ideology.

Other women's organizations followed. In 1986 Zahra Mostafavi, Khomeini's daughter, established the Women's Committee of the Islamic Republic of Iran. The following year, the government set up the Women's Social and Cultural Council to advise the government regarding women's issues. Majlis member Maryam Behruzi was one of the women selected for the council.

Although committed to the regime, Behruzi was vocal in fighting for women. In a major speech in the Majlis in February 1982, she had advised Iranian women to speak out. "Strive to counter the atmosphere that has been created against you, in order to drive you out of public life," she said. "Don't be put off by the deeds of a bunch of Godless hypocrites who testify to an imaginary Islam when it suits their purposes and turn their back on it otherwise. The rules and the law of Islam are all just, and as the Imam says: women have more rights than men."

In 1987 Behruzi created a conservative women's group called the Zainab Society, a political party based on the principle that in Islam men and women are equal. The society trained women to participate in politics and to lobby both Majlis deputies and religious leaders on women's issues. It took its motto from a quotation by Ayatollah Khomeini: "Women should not assume that they can sit home and let men do the work. Everyone, wherever he/she is, should work to improve his/her community."

Women's publications took the same approach, defending Islamic codes of behavior while arguing for women's rights. In 1980 Azam Taleqani, a Majlis deputy and a daughter of Ayatollah Taleqani, started a woman's newspaper called *Payam-e Hajar* (The Message of Hagar). In Muslim, Christian, and Jewish tradition, Hagar was the mother of

Ishmael, who is considered the founding father of the Ishmaelites, or Arabs. Hagar's loving care for her infant son in the Arabian Desert made her a symbol of motherhood. Articles in Taleqani's newspaper criticized Iran's family laws and polygamy.

The Islamic government also allowed the revival of the women's magazine *Zan-e Ruz* (Today's Woman). During the shah's regime, this magazine had provided women with housekeeping and beauty tips. The new content reflected the new order. While upholding Islamic ideals, the magazine questioned the regime's policies toward women. By telling stories of poor widows left homeless by inheritance laws, divorcees losing children to the custody of drug-addicted ex-husbands, and wives driven to suicide by violent husbands, the articles called attention to the injustices of the family laws. The magazine also highlighted the difficulties women faced in getting jobs.

The regime responded by requiring *Today's Woman* to carry more articles by clergy. Since magazines depended on the government to subsidize the cost of newsprint, the editor had to agree or close.

Activists also wrote letters to newspapers, expressing their views. One such letter argued that instead of compulsory chadors for women, the government should require modest clothing for both men and women, to be enforced by lawful means, not by vigilantes. As women had found in the early 1900s, letters to newspapers offered a safer means of speaking out than public demonstrations.

■ WOMEN'S EDUCATION

In spite of the war during the 1980s, the Islamic Republic spent more on education than on defense. The aim was to teach students to support a government based on religion and led by clergy (sometimes referred to as a theocracy). Religious scholars Islamicized the curriculum, or revised it to emphasize Islam. Rewritten textbooks passed over Iran's long history of secular monarchs in favor of the arrival of Islam and the lives of the prophet Muhammad and the twelve imams of the Shia faith. Illustrations in schoolbooks showed men and women wearing Islamic dress. The names of the characters in children's books were changed from Persian names such as Pari and Javed to Islamic names such as Ali, Hussein, and Zahra. The government closed the universities for two years while it reorganized the courses and fired faculty who disagreed with the changes.

The educational losses for women, especially women from upper-class families, were great. Organized sports were the first to go, since gender separation policies did not allow women to be coached by men or to compete publicly with men present. The policies also forbade music and drama, not just for women but for everyone. Girls could no longer study science and mathematics in high school because not enough women taught those subjects and too few women students applied to justify separate classes. In the universities, women were barred from studying law and many technical subjects. According to one count, women were denied access to 140 different fields of study.

But the new policies helped some women. In 1979, 62 percent of Iranian women could not read or write. After the revolution, the regime built schools in villages and rural areas. Religious families grew more comfortable with allowing their daughters to attend school. An army of volunteers, many of them women, taught literacy classes in remote areas and in city slums. The literacy rate, especially for poor, working-class, and traditional women, shot up.

More schools specifically for women came into being. Farah Pahlavi University was Islamicized and its name was changed to Al-Zahra University. In Qom, Iran's chief center of religious study, a seminary (religious school) for women opened in 1985. "Now that more women are on the path to becoming an ayatollah, the revolution is introducing real equality," an instructor asserted.

By 1989 lobbying by the Women's Social and Cultural Council had lifted many of the restrictions on women's education. The numbers of women attending universities rose, preparing more women for the workforce and bringing new momentum and direction to the women's movement.

CHAPTER 7

GAINS
AND
LOSSES

"Women constitute half the population of every country. To disregard women and bar them from active participation in political, social, economic and cultural life would in fact be tantamount [equivalent] to depriving the entire population of every society of half its capacity."

—Iranian lawyer Shirin Ebadi, Nobel Peace Prize acceptance speech, December 10, 2003

Ten years after the revolution, Iran entered a new phase.
The war with Iraq ended in 1988 with no clear winner, and Ayatollah
Khomeini died the following year. Yet even without its founder, the
Islamic Republic survived. A new Supreme Leader and a new president
were in office, ready to carry on the goals of the revolution.

Khomeini's successor, Ali Khamenei, was a devoted follower of
the Imam. As a conservative cleric, he had been jailed four times by
the shah. After the revolution he served two terms as president of the
Islamic Republic, from 1981 to 1989.

Khamenei was not a high-ranking cleric, however, nor was he
known for his scholarship. Although he was quickly promoted to
ayatollah to enhance his status, he did not command the reverence
and respect that the clergy and devout Shias had had for Khomeini.

**Crowds of mourners pay their respects to Ayatollah Khomeini as his body
lies in state at Martyr's Cemetery in Tehran in June 1989.**

The new president, Ali Akbar Hashemi Rafsanjani, was also a mid-ranking conservative cleric. He had organized militant supporters of Khomeini during the Imam's exile and served on the Revolutionary Council after Khomeini's return. A capable politician, he was speaker (leader) of the Majlis during the 1980s. As president, he set about replacing hard-line Islamists with experienced managers who knew how to run the government and the economy more efficiently.

■ ■ ■ ■ A MORE MODERATE THEOCRACY

Rafsanjani's leadership shifted the focus away from strict observance of religious social codes and toward improving the material well-being of Iranians. He encouraged industry, foreign trade, and investment. Although he was a firm believer in patriarchy, his economic programs held a number of side benefits for women.

Of Rafsanjani's varied measures to improve the well-being of the people, the introduction of birth control was among the most successful—and the most beneficial to women. During the 1980s, when birth control had been banned and motherhood promoted, Iran's population shot up. The number of children born to the average woman rose to seven, an all-time high for Iran.

To curb the runaway population growth, the government opened health houses especially for women. The houses distributed free contraceptives (birth control). The government also cut money grants that encouraged large families, added sex education to the school curriculum, and required newlyweds to attend family planning classes. Billboards featured families of four—mom, dad, and two kids. Clergy preached the virtues of family planning in mosques and on radio and television.

The program also addressed other women's issues. To discourage polygamy, the program advised women to have their husbands sign marriage contracts promising not to take second wives. To make it easier, the government supplied engaged couples with contracts including this demand. The contracts also offered the option of dividing property equally in case of divorce. Iranian feminists would have preferred to see polygamy banned outright and divorce laws made more equal. However, these measures at least helped women secure monogamous marriages and, if divorced, a fair distribution of property.

The birth control program was wildly successful. By the mid-1990s, the number of children born to the average woman had dropped to three. Another major benefit for women was the recruitment of thousands of volunteer housewives to staff the health houses and bring family planning to poor neighborhoods, small villages, and rural areas. The work involved them in their communities and led many to become activists for other local improvements. In 1999, when the first local elections were held, hundreds of these workers boldly ran for office.

In another cost-cutting measure, in 1991 the government merged the neighborhood komitehs, which had enforced social codes, with the police. The result was a more relaxed approach to morality laws. Women began getting by with a little modest lipstick, pale nail polish, and filmy headscarves. Fewer cars were stopped and searched, and fewer private parties were disrupted.

■ ■ ■ POLITICAL GAINS FOR WOMEN

In the Majlis, women deputies continued to press for legal changes. The number of women deputies jumped to nine in 1992 and to fourteen in 1996. But they were still a tiny minority in the 270-member body.

The women deputies also faced condescension and outright opposition from many of their male colleagues. In 1996 Faezeh Hashemi, the younger daughter of President Rafsanjani, won the largest number of votes in the Majlis election. This should have made her speaker of the Majlis. Instead, after a hasty recount, the Majlis decided that a male candidate, conservative cleric Ali Akbar Nateq-Nouri, had won the most votes, and he became the speaker.

The women deputies differed politically. Yet they worked together on women's issues to achieve a number of small gains in employment and marriage laws. One measure linked the bridal gift (or dowry) to the inflation rate. That way, if the wife wished to collect her dowry years later, it would not have decreased in value from the time of the marriage, when she was promised the gift. Another law allowed the mother custody of a child whose physical or mental health was in danger following a divorce. A third law allowed women to become legal consultants in Iran's courts. It was a first step toward putting women back into the courtroom.

In the fifth Majlis (1996–2000), however, for the first time women deputies split over issues that concerned women. One of the most controversial was the proposal by Dr. Marzieh Vahid Dastjerdi, a gynecologist and a conservative woman deputy, that men's and women's health care be totally segregated. The law would prohibit male doctors and nurses from treating women patients. This meant that new women doctors would have to be trained. Faezeh Hashemi was among the women deputies opposing the bill. The long-term benefits of having more women doctors could not outbalance the short-term risks to women when women doctors might not be available because they were not yet trained. The bill passed the Majlis, but it was rejected by the Guardian Council for the high costs involved.

Dastjerdi also actively pushed for another measure that divided the women deputies. It was an amendment to a 1990 press law that outlined the duties of newspapers and other media. This new measure banned the "promotion of conflict between men and women through defense of women's rights outside of the law and Sharia." The measure was clearly aimed at curbing articles in favor of women's rights. Dastjerdi vigorously defended the

Faezeh Hashemi, daughter of president Ali Akbar Hashemi Rafsanjani, was elected to the Majlis in 1996. As a deputy, she worked for women's rights.

amendment as designed to protect women's status and honor, adding threats to "deal with" those opposed to it. The bill became law in 1998.

"I used to think that the presence of any woman in the Majlis, regardless of leaning or viewpoint, is to the benefit of women," Faezeh Hashemi told a group of women activists later. "But now I believe that their perspective and outlook are extremely important, and we must be aware of this."

Meanwhile, women were making small advances into the upper ranks of government. In 1995 the Ministry of Justice hired one hundred women lawyers to act as legal consultants. Three years later, it appointed four women to investigate cases and advise the clerics sitting as judges in special civil courts. Women could still not issue rulings, but at least the government saw the need for their expertise. The Ministry of Health appointed the Islamic Republic's first woman deputy minister in 1995. It was the highest position a woman had achieved in the civil service a since the revolution.

The government also set up women's affairs committees in a number of ministries to advise ministers on women's issues. These committees also took steps to improve women's lives. The women's affairs committee of the Ministry of the Interior, for example, set up free marriage guidance and vocational classes.

Emboldened by the hope that women were at last gaining ground in government, in 1997 nine women threw their hats into the ring for the presidency. The Guardian Council promptly tossed them back. None were allowed to run. But this effort raised the issue for debate. As one of the would-be candidates, former Majlis deputy Azam Taleqani said, "I didn't want to become president. I didn't have any claim on the job. What I wanted to do was seize an opportunity, to crystallize the issue in the mind of the nation."

WOMEN'S VOICES

Women inside and outside the government continued using the press to make their voices heard. In 1990 the Women's Committee of the Islamic Republic of Iran published its first magazine, *Neda* (The Calling).

Like *The Message of Hagar*, it supported the regime while seeking more rights for women within it.

Popular magazines such as *Today's Woman* continued to cover many social issues of concern to women. But censors ensured that nothing criticizing the regime or promoting women's rights appeared in print.

In 1992 Shahla Sherkat, tired of the clerical meddling in editorial matters, left her post as editor of *Today's Woman* and started a bold new magazine, *Zanan* (Women). It carried a wide variety of articles. Short stories and essays by internationally known women writers appeared next to pieces on health and cooking and interviews with politicians, women filmmakers, and television stars.

Among these less provocative topics, the editors slipped in controversial ones, such as prostitution and polygamy. They also reported in depth on women's careers and family lives and nudged the regime with opinion polls on political issues. But it kept a nonpolitical, objective tone.

The first issue featured an article on women's employment. It noted that in 1989 only 5 percent of the professional jobs in Iran were held by women. In the next issue, a sociologist at Tehran University pointed out that women made up only 12 percent of civil service employees. "Women have been rejected from administrative positions," she concluded. "Increasingly, the most suitable and best environment for women of any educational level has become the home."

Sherkat's tactics worked well. By not openly challenging the regime, she managed to keep women informed about important women's issues. Censors left *Women* alone for the most part. The government occasionally denied the magazine money for the paper it was printed on when it felt Sherkat had crossed an undefined line.

In 1998 Faezeh Hashemi began *Zan* (Woman), Iran's first daily newspaper for women. She said she launched it out of frustration with the slow progress on women's issues in the Majlis. Like *Women*, *Woman* featured surveys of women's views, but it argued more openly against laws that were unfair to women.

An office worker looks at the first issue of *Woman*, an Iranian daily newspaper started by Faezeh Hashemi in 1998.

COPING WITH CHANGE

Some Iranian women regained a sense of purpose in the 1990s. These were not "regime women," such as the daughters and wives of clerics and merchants who came from traditional religious backgrounds. Nor were they the poor and working-class women who were able to rise in status in the new regime because of the expansion of women's education. They were from the educated, upper and middle classes. Most had supported the revolution but not its takeover by religious fundamentalists. They were secularists who believed that religion and politics belonged in separate spheres.

In many ways, the revolution had hurt these women most. Some had held important positions under the shah. They had lost friends, family, and colleagues who had escaped into exile or who had been executed by the revolutionaries. They had lost many freedoms that they had fought for and won under the shah—the right to work, the right to divorce, the right to wear what they pleased. Most had lost their careers. Yet they chose to stay in their homeland.

To survive, these women had had to restructure their lives. One, a librarian fired during the Islamization of the universities, became a seamstress. She managed to save enough money to open a successful bookstore.

Working from home was a frequent solution. Women started home-based businesses selling clothing or art; teaching yoga, dance, or aerobics; or tutoring children. Pari Zanganeh, a popular folksinger, had been banned from public performances after the revolution. For years she gave private singing lessons to support herself. In the 1990s, the Ministry of Culture and Islamic Guidance finally allowed her to hold concerts in her home, for women audiences only.

Shirin Ebadi took early retirement in 1984 rather than continue working with the regime. At first she wrote books and articles. In 1992 she started a private law practice. But she was appalled to discover that most cases were resolved by bribes. She decided to do only pro bono work (free services for a good cause), focusing on defending victims of the regime, especially women and children. That way, she decided, "I could at least showcase the injustice of the Islamic Republic's laws." Her work gained international attention. In February 1997, she received an award from Human Rights Watch, an international organization dedicated to protecting the human rights of people around the world. Just has she had hoped, she had found a way to fight the regime by calling attention to its crimes.

In 1999 Ebadi spoke philosophically of the loss of her position as a judge. "I believe that for every bad situation there's always a positive side. If the revolution had not happened I'd never have become a writer. If there'd not been a revolution, the most I could have achieved was to have become minister of justice, but because of the revolution I've become a fighter and I'm alive."

Her fellow lawyer Mehrangiz Kar followed a similar course. She defended human rights cases in court, published books, and wrote articles for *Women* and other magazines on the impact of Iran's civil laws on the lives of women.

BECOMING VISIBLE

Women were becoming visible in other ways. The number of women working outside the home in Iran was once again rising. The total share of women in the workforce in 1996 almost matched the share in 1976. By 2006 it had inched past 1976 levels. It was not just a change in numbers. In the 1970s, many women had had professional careers. But the vast majority had labored in carpet factories and on farms. During the 1990s, the balance shifted dramatically. Fewer women workers remained trapped in low-paying, unskilled jobs. Far more were becoming secretaries, teachers, doctors, nurses, engineers, publishers, television newscasters, writers, researchers, and computer technicians.

One reason for this change was that women were gaining educationally. Government spending on education remained high. As educational restrictions lifted, women began taking advantage of the chance to study engineering, science, and technology. In 1993 the government opened a medical school for women in Qom. With 95 percent of Iranian girls attending primary school, the gap between men's and women's education narrowed. By 1998 more than one-third of university faculty and 40 percent of university students were women.

Women also were playing sports. The Islamic Revolution had put an end to organized sports for women. For women to exercise in public was deemed un-Islamic. Most of Iran's sports facilities had been closed or handed over to men. Women athletes were dropped from Iran's Olympic teams. Failing to get attention from the regime, Iran's sportswomen found help from Faezeh Hashemi. With her close ties to the government, Hashemi was able to persuade officials of the health benefits of sports for women.

Gradually, some sports facilities allowed women to use their space when men were not there. A few parks banned men for several hours each week to allow women to run. One park in Tehran opened a women-only bicycle path. In the late 1990s, groups of women in scarves and long, loose-fitting tunics called *roopooshes* began to gather in city parks for early morning calisthenics (exercise). They looked, one reporter said, "like a flock of ravens about to take flight."

Women's gyms opened. Some were fancy private clubs in upscale neighborhoods, but others were government-run recreation centers open to all women. They offered many facilities—swimming pools, weight rooms, indoor ball courts, treadmills, and other exercise machines.

For Iranian women athletes to take part in international competitions, however, was more complicated. Not too many sports can be performed in a chador. Aware that women in other Muslim countries faced similar restrictions, Hashemi came up with the idea of an international sports competition for Muslim women. In 1993 Tehran hosted the first Women's Islamic Games. Ten countries sent teams. Men were banished from the stands so that track stars could perform in Lycra shorts. No cameras recorded the games. "This is nice for us," said a woman athlete who competed in the first games. "Our way of thinking, our culture is this way. It would be hard for us, now, to compete in front of men." Held every four years, the games have attracted more and more Muslim women athletes. Forty-four countries sent squads in 2005. Future games will take place when construction is completed on a new women-only stadium in Tehran.

Since 1996 Iranian women have also taken part in the Olympics. Their sports are limited to ones that can be performed in clothing that covers all but the hands and face. Iranian women athletes have competed in Olympic archery, shooting, rowing, tae kwan do, and skiing. As the first Iranian woman to take part in the Winter Olympics, skier Marjan Kahlor beamed with happiness even when she finished last in both her

Marjan Kahlor competed for Iran in the 2010 Winter Olympics in Vancouver, British Columbia, Canada. She was the first Iranian woman to take part in the Winter Olympics.

races in Vancouver, Canada, in 2010. "It was really okay," she said. "I'm the first one. [Iranian women skiers] will practice and will be much better in the next Olympics."

■ ■ ■ A NEW ERA

The most promising event for Iranian women since the revolution was the 1997 presidential election. The Guardian Council allowed four candidates to compete. The speaker of the Majlis, Ali Akbar Nateq-Nouri, who had the backing of all the conservative parties, was expected to succeed Rafsanjani. But the Guardian Council underestimated the appeal of Mohammad Khatami, a mid-ranking cleric who was an administrator at the National Library.

Khatami had served as minister of culture and Islamic guidance for ten years. But he was forced to resign in 1992 for defending the freedom of speech of a prominent filmmaker who had angered the clerics. Khatami's platform emphasized the need for dialogue, respect for the opinions of others, and rule of law, not force. His views attracted liberals, women, and young people. Even conservative women were drawn to his progressive views of Sharia law. His unpretentious, smiling manner didn't hurt.

On election day, a near-record number of voters turned out. In a surprise landslide win, Khatami captured almost 70 percent of the vote. His victory set the ball rolling for reform. Iranians hoped for more freedom of speech and of the press, more political diversity, and a more open society. For a brief window

Iranian presidential candidate Mohammad Khatami won 70 percent of the vote in 1997.

of time, Iranians envisioned an Iran that would be both Islamic and democratic. Women believed that they had reached a turning point in their battle for equal rights.

Khatami had a full agenda of reform to attend to, but he did not neglect women. He appointed the first woman vice president in Iran's history, Massoumeh Ebtekar. (She had acted as spokesperson for the students occupying the U.S. Embassy in 1979.) She took charge of environmental issues in Khatami's cabinet. He raised his adviser of women's affairs to a higher-level position as a cabinet member. For the first time since the 1970s, two women served in Iran's cabinet. In 1999 the president appointed the feminist author Zahra Rahnavard to lead Al-Zahra University, the prestigious women-only academic center in Tehran. She was the first Iranian woman to be a college president.

Two other elections bolstered hope for women and for the reform movement. In 1999 the Islamic Republic held its first local elections since the revolution. Candidates who supported reform won 75 percent of the vote. Five thousand women ran for seats on city councils. They won more than three hundred places. That was almost as many women city council members as Iran had had before the revolution.

In the 2000 Majlis elections, huge crowds turned out. About 84 percent of eligible voters went to the polls. They elected reform

"The traditional outlook, based on the erroneous [false] notion of superiority of men over women, does injustice to men, women, and humanity as a whole. We should recognize that both men and women are valuable components of humanity that equally possess the potential for intellectual, social, cultural, and political development."

—Iranian President Mohammad Khatami, *speaking on the opening day of the Fifty-Third United Nations General Assembly, New York City, September 21, 1998*

candidates to 80 percent of the seats. The number of women deputies slipped down to thirteen. But for the first time, significant numbers of their male colleagues were willing to vote for women's rights. In another first, a woman was elected to the presiding board of the Majlis. The presiding board is important because it determines the number of members on each of twenty-three standing committees and appoints other committees to meet special needs.

■ ■ ■ WORK FOR CHANGE

After the February 2000 Majlis elections, Iranian reformist leaders met during a conference in Berlin, Germany, to discuss plans. Several Iranian feminists took part in the conference. They included *Women* editor Shahla Sherkat, women's rights lawyer Mehrangiz Kar, and publisher Shahla Lahiji. The conference had been approved by the government, but televised reports of its proceedings brought conservative objections. When the reformists returned to Tehran, security forces arrested ten of them at the airport. The courts charged them with "acting against the internal security of the state" and "disparaging the holy order of the Islamic Republic."[12]

Three feminists were among those arrested. Sherkat received a public trial and was fined for her part in the conference. Kar and Lahiji, however, were treated more severely. They were each subjected to secret trials and two months in prison.

The arrests sparked the formation of the first government-sanctioned independent women's organization in the Islamic Republic, the Women's Cultural Center. Women activists founded the center on International Women's Day, March 8, 2001. Its women's studies library created a welcome space for women to gather and plan ways to combat patriarchal laws and customs. Many more women's organizations followed. Most sought to involve young women in seeking their rights. According to Mahboubeh Abbasgholizadeh, who helped train groups of activists, they were "a way for these girls to express their own identity, to announce, 'I'm here.'"

The reformist Majlis granted many feminists' demands. One bill erased all distinctions between men and women regarding the testimony of witnesses in court and monetary awards for damages. Another restored women's right to be appointed judges. A third gave women equal rights in divorce courts. Single women were finally permitted to study abroad on state scholarships. Even dress codes were slightly modified. Schoolgirls received permission to wear colorful clothes to school and women deputies to wear headscarves instead of chadors during Majlis sessions. It was a giant leap forward for women.

Most amazing of all, in 2003, the Majlis voted for ratifying the United Nations Convention on the Elimination of All Forms of Discrimination against Women (CEDAW). This statement of women's rights was adopted by the UN General Assembly in 1979 as an international bill of rights for women. Its thirty articles define ways in which women are discriminated against and set an agenda for each nation to eliminate such discrimination. Both Khomeini and Khamenei had vigorously opposed ratifying CEDAW.

■ ■ ■ THE CONSERVATIVES HIT BACK

Almost none of the Majlis reforms became law. The Guardian Council rejected all the bills related to women and family as incompatible with Islamic law. Others they trimmed or gutted. One Majlis bill raised the legal marriage age for girls to eighteen. The Council cut it back to thirteen. It also annulled the ratification of CEDAW.

The Council refused numerous other bills related to human rights. Bans on torture and secret trials were vetoed. So was a law requiring legal counsel for political prisoners. An attempt to stop the Guardian Council from vetting election candidates also failed.

It wasn't just the Guardian Council. The judiciary joined the conservative backlash by closing down some sixty reformist periodicals. People called it "the great newspaper massacre."

Many journalists, historians, and other writers were arrested. The charges included apostasy (renouncing one's religion), disturbing public opinion, insulting Islam, and endangering national security.

Among the victims was Faezeh Hashemi's women's newspaper

Woman. To illustrate the unequal value the law put on men's and women's lives, she had published a cartoon showing a couple being held up by an armed robber. The man says "Don't shoot me, shoot my wife! That way you'll only have to pay the family half as much!" The joke went too far for the censors. Accusing Hashemi of ridiculing Islam, the censors shut *Woman* down in 1999.

Another loss was *The Message of Hagar*. After the Guardian Council rejected Azam Taleqani's candidacy for the presidency, she interviewed a number of ayatollahs. Several told her that there was no religious reason why a woman should not hold the office of president. When Taleqani published their answers in *The Message of Hagar*, the courts banned that magazine too. Taleqani herself was too prominent to prosecute, but some of her women coworkers were arrested.

A woman filmmaker was also challenged. In 2001 Tahmineh Milani directed *The Hidden Half*, a movie about an Iranian woman with a secret political life. The Ministry of Culture and Islamic Guidance approved the script. But after the film's release, the police arrested Milani on grounds of "abusing the arts as a tool for supporting counter-revolutionary groups." It was a serious charge. If found guilty, she would be sentenced to execution. In the end, Khatami personally intervened. After Milani's release, Khatami told reporters that the arrest "shouldn't have happened." The judiciary had no right to censor a film passed by the Ministry of Culture, he said.

The Revolutionary Guard, the police, and the *Basij* (a volunteer militia under the Revolutionary Guard) added their troops to the war on reform. Among the bloodiest encounters were riots that broke out during the summer of 1999. In retaliation for a student protest against the closing of a popular reformist newspaper, basijis and police invaded the campus of Tehran University and beat students in their dorms. The violent assault triggered a week of clashes that spread to other cities.

Shirin Ebadi investigated the violence for the family of a student killed in the dorm attack. Her effort landed her in prison. She served twenty-five days, much of it in solitary confinement. In the end, the court simply dismissed her case and that of the dead student. None of the attackers were brought to justice.

The 1990s brought a flowering of Iranian culture. Artists, writers, actors, and filmmakers all benefited from the brief shift to more moderate and liberal politics. Book production expanded fourfold, and women publishers such as Shahla Lahiji were at the forefront of the wave. Women's issues were topics of major interest. A popular item was Noushin Ahmadi Khorasani's annual calendar devoted to keeping the history of women in Iran alive.

Women also got behind cameras to make films that put women's social and legal problems in the spotlight. Rakhshan Bani-Etemad was the first woman filmmaker to deal with the Iran-Iraq War and the devastating effects of war on women. Her films also probe the complex relationships of mothers and children and the issues of divorce and polygamy. Tahmineh Milani's popular and controversial film *Two Women* (1999) contrasts the lives of friends who are separated when one is forced to marry a jealous man.

Many women's documentaries and dramas based on real events give an inside view of women's lives in Iran. Mehrangiz Kar and British director Kim Longinotto teamed up to film *Divorce Iranian Style* (1998), a documentary about several cases in an Iranian divorce court. Sociologist Shahla Haeri's film *Mrs. President* (2001) documented women's efforts to become presidential candidates. Manijeh Hekmat's *Women's Prison* (2002) showed women's experiences in jail. Two films by women focused on the 2009 presidential elections. Hana Makhmalbaf's *Green Days* (2009) used footage of the demonstrations after the elections to tell a fictional story. Bani-Etemad interviewed candidates for their positions on women's rights in *We Are Half of Iran's Population* (2009).

These were just some of the constant battles faced by Khatami and the reform movement. It was increasingly clear that the reforms Khatami had hoped to achieve could not prevail against the hard-line conservatives. For women, the situation was especially discouraging. With no freedom of speech, the press, or assembly, there was little chance for progress in the struggle for women's rights.

One bright beacon of hope came from overseas. In October 2003, Shirin Ebadi was at a film conference in Paris when news reached

Iranian activist Shirin Ebadi *(right)* received the Nobel Peace Prize in 2003 for her work for women's rights in her country.

her that she had been awarded the Nobel Peace Prize. Thousands of women in white headscarves crowded Tehran's airport to welcome her return. All of the women Majlis deputies met her as she left the plane. Khomeini's granddaughter Zahra Eshragi placed a garland of flowers around Ebadi's neck. The conservative clergy thundered against the prize as a foreign threat to undermine Islam. But women's spirits were buoyed to know that people in other parts of the world were applauding their struggle.

Ebadi's colleague Mehrangiz Kar received a Human Rights Award from Human Rights First, an international humanitarian organization, the following year. In her acceptance speech, she emphasized the courage and perseverance of Iranian women. "If the last two decades of pain indicate how women will react when faced with turmoil," she said, "then we do not have to worry, for we have met strife with determined spirits."

CHAPTER 8

WOMEN
UNITE

"Women's rights will be fulfilled only
when the constitution changes."

—Mahboubeh Abbasgholizadeh, Iranian feminist leader, June 12, 2005

In 2000 Iran's women activists began planning a new tack. One problem all along had been a split between the old guard—the women who had been part of the women's movement before the revolution—and the women who came to power with the revolution. Many of the women of the revolutionary regime were wives and daughters of high-ranking clerics. They took up politics during the revolution and remained active when the clerics took control of the new government. Azam Taleqani and Faezeh Hashemi were among these women. Others came from more moderate religious backgrounds. Through the expansion of girls' education, they had become actively interested in women's rights.

Azam Taleqani was a member of the Majlis and founder of a woman's newspaper critical of Iran's family laws. Here she answers questions during a 2005 press conference in Tehran.

The old guard and the regime women are often spoken of respectively as secular and religious. These terms, however, can be misleading. The "secular" women are not antireligion. They support the idea of a secular government and freedom of religion. They see religious belief as a private matter. The "religious" women activists support the Islamic government. But they do not agree with the conservative religious views of the ruling clergy. They believe religious laws may be interpreted in ways more appropriate to modern society.

In January 2000, a group of secular women, among them Shirin Ebadi and Mehrangiz Kar, invited the religious regime women members of the fifth Majlis to a meeting. The idea was to analyze and discuss how women deputies could achieve better results. It was an unheard of face-to-face meeting between these two groups.

Only three of the fourteen Majlis members showed up, but it was a productive encounter. The secular women vented their frustrations at the lack of change. Kar wanted to know why the law allowed a girl of nine to be punished as an adult. Ebadi asked, "Is it really an honor to have a female vice-president who, when she wants to leave the country, must bow her head to her husband and ask him for permission?"

The deputies defended their accomplishments, however small, and decried the lack of media coverage for their efforts. But, one admitted that had they met sooner, "maybe we would have taken you into account more."

The forum produced no road map to equal rights. But it brought together two very different and separate groups for the first time. As each side shared its frustrations, the gap between them narrowed, and the idea of joining forces soon took root.

■ ■ ■ CONSERVATIVES TAKE CHARGE

In the 2003 local elections, conservatives rebounded. The following year, the Guardian Council vetted the Majlis candidates more strictly than before. Hundreds of reformist candidates, including those already in office, were not allowed to run. Only two of the women deputies passed the Guardian Council's net. When Fatemeh Haqiqatioo, the youngest and one of the most outspoken of the women deputies, heard she could not run for reelection, she decided to resign. Referring to the Guardian Council as "power-drunk opponents of the popular vote," she argued that reform from within the system was no longer possible. "The possibility of keeping my oath [to serve the people] has been taken from me," she said.

Many women boycotted the 2004 Majlis elections in protest. As one young woman told lawyer and journalist Shadi Sadr, "There was no candidate left that I could vote for."

After the election, the number of women deputies held almost steady at twelve. But they differed from the women who had served before. Ten of the eleven new women members belonged to the conservative Zainab Society. Only one previous deputy was reelected.

In one of their first acts, the deputies showed their support for gender segregation. The women of the reform Majlis (2000-2004) had taken down the curtain separating the women's lunch space from that of their male colleagues. The new deputies hung it back up.

One of the new deputies told journalists that the idea of legal rights was imported from the West and should be eliminated from public discussion in Iran. People should not think about their rights, she said, but about their religious duties. She also asserted that polygamy benefits women.

Another new woman deputy called for filtering the Internet to prevent Western ideas from spreading in Iran. Several of the women deputies expressed opposition to passage of the UN's CEDAW proclamation, declaring its criteria un-Islamic. No battle for women's rights was going to occur in the seventh Majlis. As one new deputy said, "Bringing up the issue of gender justice is a case of bullying men."

■ ■ ■ WHAT NEXT?

The loss of feminist representatives in the Majlis forced women activists to come up with new ways to assert their rights. The women leaders who had served as deputies in the reform Majlis began to feel a kinship with the secular women, who had been out in the cold since the revolution. After twenty-four years of trying to work within the system, religious feminists saw that their biggest obstacle was the constitution.

The way the government worked gave little hope for change, even if a majority of the Iranian people wanted it. A committee appointed by the Supreme Leader and the judiciary chose the candidates. Laws passed by elected legislators could be vetoed by the same committee. The conservative patriarchy was well entrenched.

Still, the constitution did guarantee the right of peaceful assembly, even though local laws required a permit for public meetings. Women began testing the limits by holding small rallies in parks. For International Women's Day in 2003, the Women's Cultural Center planned a gathering in Laleh Park in central Tehran instead of a small indoor meeting. About 150 women and men came with banners

Women gather in Laleh Park in Tehran in 2004 for a demonstration protesting violations of their rights. The women were under close watch by authorities as they gathered.

protesting violations of women's rights. They resisted police orders to disperse. The following year, feminists met more opposition at a similar event. This time basijis showed up and beat people with batons. Police arrested several participants.

EQUAL RIGHTS IS OUR MINIMUM DEMAND

In the summer of 2004, women's groups in Iran began planning a large, unauthorized demonstration. They worked for a year to bring together diverse groups from all over the nation. A new bimonthly online journal *Zanestan* (Women's City) was launched to coordinate and publicize the event. Deciding that backing one politician or another was not the answer, feminist leaders honed in on the real problem: the constitution itself. It had to guarantee equal rights to women.

In November 2004, the arrest of Mahboubeh Abbasgholizadeh added to the feminists' determination to act. Abbasgholizadeh trained women to form feminist organizations, edited a women's studies journal, and contributed articles to reformist websites. Because no charges were made, it was never clear which of her activities had crossed the line. After she spent thirty days in prison, pressure from within Iran and from abroad brought about her release. The arrest was a warning to feminists that the government would deal harshly with them. But that wasn't going to stop them.

Organizers decided that the best time for the large demonstration would be just before the presidential election in June 2005. The presence of many foreign journalists in Iran to cover the election would make the protest safer for the women. They also hoped it would give the women's movement the chance to reach a wider public abroad.

Several thousand women crowded the open area in front of Tehran University's main gates on June 12, 2005. It was the first large public demonstration by women since the 1979 protest marches. More than ninety women's groups took part. They represented a wide spectrum of political and religious views. Student and environmentalist groups added their support. Many men who supported the women stood politely and protectively on the edges of the crowd.

> "Women began to move!
> They sang as they walked.
> Demanding their rights,
> They sang as police brutalized them."
>
> —from a poem by Iranian writer Simin Behbahani,
> read by her at the June 12, 2005, demonstration in Tehran

An army of security forces soon marched in and tried to intimidate the women into leaving. With great courage, the sea of women in brightly colored headscarves sat on the ground and refused to move. They chanted, "We are women, we are the children of this land, but we have no rights" and "Equal rights is our minimum demand." In the end, the security forces gave up trying to disperse the demonstration.

People listened to speeches about women's rights, to Simin Behbahani's poem, and to a message from Shirin Ebadi. They joined in singing "Women's Freedom," a protest song that Noushin Ahmadi Khorasani had written for the occasion.

Poet Simin Behbahani waits for her chance to deliver her poem during the rally for women's rights in front of Tehran University in June 2005.

The organizers agreed it was a great day. Planning the sit-in had linked different groups of women, established a communications network, and helped the women articulate their demands. Their effort had also won the support of international agencies and human rights activists outside Iran. Such support, Khorasani noted, "gave us a sense of security and confidence to go ahead and overcome the fear of arrest."

Not all of Iran's leading women's activists took part in the sit-in. Azam Taleqani did not come. She had organized her own, smaller sit-in on June 1 to protest the exclusion of women from the presidential race. She had been one of the first women to apply to run for the presidency in 1997, and she had repeated the effort in 2001 and 2005. It was still just a symbolic gesture, but one that she wished to keep in the public eye. The number of women entering their names had grown from nine in 1997 to eighty-nine in 2005. Many of them joined her demonstration.

Also not present were several former women deputies who belonged to the Islamic Iran Participation Front (IIPF). For them, not attending was a political decision. The male IIPF leaders believed that the struggle for democracy should have priority over the struggle for women's rights. The women who organized the rally did not agree. Women's rights were essential to democracy, they believed, and a step toward it. The statement read at the June protest declared, "Democracy cannot be achieved without freedom and equal rights." The tension between reformists and feminists, however, was unfortunate. To split into factions would not help either side.

■ ■ ■ ANOTHER HARD-LINE CONSERVATIVE WIN

Large numbers of Iranian women and reformists stayed away from the polls in June 2005. Barely 60 percent of eligible voters turned out. Many felt that it was hardly worth showing up. Former president Ali Akbar Hashemi Rafsanjani was sure to win. He did, but with seven candidates running, he missed winning a majority. So Rafsanjani faced Mahmoud Ahmadinejad, the hard-line conservative candidate, in the runoff. Ahmadinejad had only won 19.5 percent of the vote in the first round of voting. Jaws dropped when, in the second round, Ahmadinejad won a landslide victory.

A former Revolutionary Guard and later a professor of civil engineering, Ahmadinejad owed his election to support from basijis and working-class people. The son of a blacksmith, he lived simply and did not belong to the clerical elite. Many voters saw him as a man of the people. His key campaign slogan was, "We shall put the fruits of oil wealth on the ordinary person's dinner table." A taxi driver explained to a visiting journalist: "Some people think that freedom means men being able to wear shorts or women to go about without the hijab. Others think that freedom means having a full belly." He paused. "There's just more of the latter." In a struggling economy, more people were worried about putting food on the table than about personal freedoms.

When Ahmadinejad came to power with a conservative-controlled Majlis to back him up, the clock turned back to the early days after the

Mahmoud Ahmadinejad (shown here in 2007) was elected president of Iran in June 2005. With his election, women's rights declined.

revolution. Proclaiming a "culture of modesty" for Iran, Ahmadinejad doubled the government's financial support of the Basij, the principal enforcers of dress and morality codes in Iran. Women basijis (about one-third of this volunteer militia) played a vital role in patrolling public places to stamp out "bad hijab."

The challenge to women's rights included legislative attacks. Majlis conservatives proposed new family laws legalizing polygamy and temporary marriage without the consent of the earlier wife and reviving stoning as the punishment for adultery. The same deputies suggested quotas (limits) on women's admissions to universities, textbook revisions to put more emphasis on women's home and family duties, and a decrease in the number of years of required public education for girls. They also called for cutting women's working hours at government agencies (along with their pay) and airing programs on TV and radio promoting polygamy and temporary marriage.

In place of Khatami's Center for Women's Participation, Ahmadinejad set up the Center for Women and Family Affairs. To counter feminism, the new center shredded publications printed by the Center for Women's Participation. It replaced them with pamphlets preaching the importance of housework and marrying young. The pamphlets blamed women activists for the nation's high unemployment rate, an increase in prostitution, and lower educational standards in the universities. Lack of modesty in women, the center's website proclaimed, endangers the "harmony of society."

Stoning is a particularly cruel form of execution. The penal code of the Islamic Republic reserves this harsh punishment as the penalty for adultery committed by married men and women, prostitution, and male homosexuality. Before the punishment begins, the condemned are buried up to their waists (if they are men) or up to their necks (if they are women). A crowd of volunteers throws stones at the condemned person. The stones must be large enough to inflict pain but not so large as to kill immediately. On average, the execution takes ten to twenty minutes. Both men and women may be subjected to stoning. But many more women receive the sentence, perhaps because they receive poorer representation in court. The practice of stoning was reintroduced in Iran soon after the Islamic Revolution in 1979 and was often carried out secretly.

In October 2006, after a man and a woman were stoned to death in Mashhad as a punishment for adultery, a group of women activists launched the Stop Stoning Forever campaign. For the first time, this secretive legal practice was exposed. Iranians and the international community reacted with horror.

The Stop Stoning campaign succeeded in capturing public opinion in Iran and around the world. In 2008 public pressure focused on eight women and one man sentenced to this death penalty. The Supreme Leader changed some of the sentences to prison terms and lashings. Others were executed by hanging. Two of the sentences, however, were upheld. The judiciary was reluctant to abolish a penalty endorsed by Islamic law, although stoning is not advocated in the Quran. The Stop Stoning campaign has been promoted by Amnesty International and other international human rights groups in Iran and other countries where stoning is a legal punishment.

When the Revolutionary Guards published the *Report on Threats to National Security* in 2006, it listed feminists (along with bloggers, secular students and intellectuals, reformists, journalists, mystics, and devil worshippers) as likely threats. Such labeling put women activists under increased security surveillance (close observation), as well as at increased risk of government-sanctioned attack by basijis.

■ ■ ■ ONWARD!

However dismayed they were by Ahmadinejad's victory, Iranian feminists vowed to continue their peaceful protests. It was no surprise, however, when they faced worse retaliation than before the election.

In early 2006, the government banned observances of International Women's Day. Some women's groups canceled planned events, but a few small indoor meetings took place without incident. One group took its chances with an outdoor commemoration in a park in central Tehran. They had barely assembled when security forces moved in and broke up the meeting. Several women were harshly beaten, among them seventy-eight-year-old poet Simin Behbahani. "I'm sad," Behbahani said later, "more for the young men that attacked the participants than for the between 300 to 400 young girls and women [who received their blows]. I don't understand the reason behind such savagery."

Plans nevertheless proceeded for a large rally in June. The idea was to commemorate two events: the Constitutional Revolution of 1906 (because women had played an important role in it) and the demonstration of 2005. Some worried that the time was not right. Such an assembly might even hurt the women's movement.

The planners posted a list of demands on the website of the online journal *Women's City*. The rally would call for an end to polygamy, equal divorce rights for men and women, joint custody of children after divorce, and equal rights for women as witnesses—in short, the abolition of gender inequalities based on conservative interpretations of Sharia law.

This time, security forces detained several leaders ahead of the protest. They warned them that any demonstration would be met with force. Fariba Davoudi Mohajer was among those summoned to court. She was subjected to ten hours of interrogation. "A social movement has its price, and [we] have to pay for it," she said later. No one called the rally off.

When women activists arrived at Haft-e Tir Square in central Tehran, a large police presence awaited them. Among the officers were numerous basiji women wearing dark police uniforms under black chadors. Police vans waited along the curb.

When the gathering group began to sing "Women's Freedom," the police moved in. The women basijis went after the women demonstrators and the policemen after the men. Wielding batons and pepper spray, they attacked the demonstrators, beat them, handcuffed them, and pulled or shoved them to the waiting vans. Arrests included forty-two women and twenty-eight men, all charged with illegal assembly. It was the first time policewomen had been used to arrest women protesters.

Female police officers, members of the Basij, attack women's rights demonstrators in Tehran in June 2006. The basijis used baton blows and other tactics to break up the gathering.

A NEW STRATEGY

It was clearly time for new tactics. The regime was fighting hard to suppress feminist ideas, and it seemed to be gaining ground. The fact that women had beaten and arrested other women who were demonstrating for rights for all women was especially galling. For the women's movement to succeed, it needed to reach all women. Given the right approach, activist women thought they could find common ground even with basiji women.

The idea that seemed most promising was a grassroots campaign in which feminists would conduct one-on-one dialogues with women from many different walks of life. They would talk to other women in the street, in the subway, or in parks. They would go door-to-door interviewing busy housewives or chat with women in beauty salons, factories, or health clubs. Everywhere they would listen to their stories, give out literature explaining the laws that discriminate against women, and ask for their signatures on a petition for legal reforms for gender equality.

The campaign would bring women from different walks of life together in a meaningful way. It would provide the opportunity for volunteers to learn about ordinary women's problems and involve women in two-way conversations about how best to bring about change.

The campaign had the further advantage of not breaking any laws. No one could arrest two women talking for illegal assembly.

COLLECTING SIGNATURES

First there was literature to prepare and volunteers to train. Organizers set to work writing a petition, a statement of goals, and a pamphlet entitled The Effect of Laws on Women's Lives for volunteers to hand out. Organizers held parties at their homes, where they trained about four hundred young women who would collect signatures. A website called Change for Equality was set up to provide information about the campaign and to enable volunteers to share their experiences and ideas.

The One Million Signatures Campaign was launched in August 2006. Organizers estimated it would take at least two years to collect that many supporters' signatures. Ebadi and other human-rights lawyers would draft proposals for specific legislation based on the priorities expressed by the signers. Once complete, the petition would be presented to the Majlis. Politicians would ignore such a petition at their peril.

The obstacles turned out to be huge. Some women were too caught up in busy lives to see anything wrong with laws that they felt did not affect them personally. Others agreed fully with the need for change but were afraid to sign their names. Or they just shrugged, believing that no petition would end discrimination against women.

Noushin Ahmadi Khorasani talked to one woman who listened but said nothing. As Khorasani was leaving, however, the woman caught up with her and showed her the bruises on her arms. "My man beats me," she said. Khorasani was left speechless. But the woman took the paper from her hands. "I am illiterate," she said. "Can you write for me?" Khorasani filled out the form for her and watched her sign with an X. The woman smiled. "God bless you," she said.

Some famous Iranians also signed on. Ayatollah Khomeini's granddaughter Zahra Eshragi added her signature in March 2007. Her action was mentioned in the Iranian press.

Whether or not Iranian women agreed with the petition, the campaign spread awareness. In the first year, one hundred thousand women signed. "We haven't achieved too many results," organizer Parvin Ardalan told a reporter. "But so far we have succeeded in changing Iranian people's attitude toward [the discriminatory] laws."

ARRESTS, TRIALS, PRISON

The biggest obstacle was the Iranian government. First it blocked the *Change for Equality* website, as well as *Women's City* and other feminist websites. The women quickly reopened the website with another name. A cyberspace game of cat and mouse began between the women and the regime. By September 2009, the government had shut down *Change for Equality* twenty-one times.

The Iranian government also prevented the campaign from renting space for seminars. All meetings had to be held secretly in members' homes. Despite the secrecy, one woman received a threatening phone call from security forces after holding a meeting in the basement of her apartment building.

Campaign members faced travel bans and the circulation of ugly rumors about their lives. Police contacted the parents of young women volunteers to urge them to advise their daughters not to participate in the campaign, saying they might be arrested.

In fact, arrests soon followed. In December 2006, a volunteer was stopped on the Tehran subway, where she was distributing pamphlets and collecting signatures. She was imprisoned for five days. Two more women were arrested, also on the subway, for carrying campaign brochures. Another two campaign workers were talking to women in Laleh Park when security forces seized them. By August 2007, thirteen volunteers for the signatures campaign had been detained. The next month, twenty-five women were arrested during a training workshop in western Iran. That fall two young volunteers were arrested in Sanandaj, the capital of the Iranian province of Kurdistan. Men who joined the effort to collect signatures were also detained.

Arrests did not let up. By November 2009, more than fifty campaign workers had been arrested. All were subjected to grueling interrogations and prison stays—some in solitary confinement—of varying lengths. Some discovered their homes ransacked and their computers confiscated. In trials held later, most were convicted. They were often sentenced to several months in prison and given two- or three-year suspended sentences. That meant that if they were arrested again, they would be imprisoned. As time went on, the sentences increased in severity. In 2008 a young woman from Iranian Kurdistan was ordered to serve a five-year prison term.

MORE ARRESTS AND TRIALS

Not all the arrests involved the signatures campaign. Some of the forty-two women arrested in the June 2006 rally faced later trials. In

March 2007, four of them were to be put on trial for "endangering national security." The court date, March 4, was probably intended to prevent any International Women's Day events. When about thirty women assembled outside the court to show their solidarity with those on trial, security forces arrested them as well. One of those arrested was later sentenced to twenty-eight months of prison for her part in the peaceful gathering. She was not intimidated. "This movement . . . will not be silenced because one or two people are in prison," she told a reporter. "Actually, women's rights activists will become more passionate and determined because one of their colleagues is behind bars."

Despite the crackdown, an outdoor rally on International Women's Day 2007 attracted about fifty demonstrators to a square near the Majlis building in Tehran. They were outnumbered by security forces. The police swarmed the square, beat several women, and detained eight. The police then sat on the pavement to prevent any regrouping. Another peaceful rally in Sanandaj also ended in arrests.

Activists took to subtler street activities. On International Women's Day in 2009, they pasted stickers with equality slogans in public spaces in several cities. Many wore T-shirts with the scientific symbol for female on the back as a conversation starter.

Besides Women's Day, activists organized the National Day of Solidarity for Iranian Women on June 12. This event is celebrated every year to mark the 2005 coming together of women's groups. Security forces, however, prevented any more large gatherings from taking place on that day. In 2008 they arrested nine women arriving at a gallery where a small event was planned. Police also harassed a group of women who went hiking in the mountains near Tehran to honor the day.

Women bloggers and writers for women's e-zines became another target of the security forces. In late 2007, the government once again shut down the *Women's City* and *Change for Equality* websites and arrested four women for their online activities. The charge was "publishing information against the government." The following September, they received mandatory prison sentences of six months.

After sixteen years of publication, Shahla Sherkat's leading women's magazine *Women* was shut down in 2008. It was a "threat to the psychological security of society," the Ministry of Culture and Islamic Guidance said, because it portrayed Iranian women in a "dark light."

In December authorities shut down Shirin Ebadi's legal assistance organization, the Center for the Defenders of Human Rights. A week later, five men from the judiciary stormed her office and confiscated her computers and documents. Security agents arrested her secretary two weeks after that. The determination to intimidate Ebadi and all other independent voices in Iran had become all too clear.

COURAGE CELEBRATED

Human rights organizations outside Iran brought world attention to Iran's women activists with awards recognizing their bravery. Parvin Ardalan, an organizer of the June 2006 rally and a founder of the signatures campaign, received the 2007 Olof Palme Award. This award, named for a Swedish statesman, honors the outstanding achievements of those who actively promote peace, equality, and security.

A presentation ceremony in Stockholm, Sweden, was slated for International Women's Day 2008. When Ardalan arrived at the Tehran airport to make the trip, however, security personnel confiscated her passport. Unable to attend in person, Ardalan sent a video of her acceptance speech. Her sister received the award for her.

It was one of many such honors. Shahla Sherkat received the Courage in Journalism Award from the International Women's Media Foundation in 2005. Human Rights First presented the 2007 Human Rights Award to journalist Fariba Davoudi Mohajer, an organizer of the June 2006 protest. In 2009 feminist poet Simin Behbahani received the Simone de Beauvoir Prize for Women's Freedom, named for the French writer and feminist. Many other Iranian women received similar awards. The recognition and the cash prizes boosted the morale and the finances of the hard-pressed women's movement.

The One Million Signatures Campaign and its website, *Change for Equality*, also won international acclaim. Reporters Without Borders,

Above: Shirin Ardalan *(right)*, sister of Iranian women's rights activist Parvin Ardalan, accepts the Olof Palme Award for Parvin in March 2008. Parvin was not allowed out of Iran to attend the ceremony. *Below*: Iranian activist and journalist Shahla Sherkat received a Courage in Journalism Award in 2005 from the International Women's Media Foundation.

an international association of journalists in support of freedom of the press and other media, honored *Change for Equality* with its Freedom of Expression award in 2009. The next year, to mark World Day against Cyber-Censorship, Reporters Without Borders and the Internet search company Google selected Iran's women bloggers of *Change for Equality* to receive the first Netizen Prize. In November 2009, *Glamour* magazine honored the founding members of the campaign as Women of the Year.

THE WHITE SCARVES

One issue that has angered many women in Iran is not being allowed to attend men's sports events, even though foreign women visiting Iran are allowed to do so. In June 2005, when Iran's soccer team was to play Bahrain's team for a chance to enter the World Cup competition, thirty women activists decided to take action.

They donned white scarves with slogans painted on them: "My share, women's share, half of freedom!" "How many steps to freedom?" "Freedom, freedom, freedom." The emphasis on freedom was a sly allusion to the name of the stadium, Azadi, which is Persian for "freedom."

First they took their tickets to the main gate. Then they tried the VIP entrance. After guards shooed them off from both these doors, they decided to rush in behind the bus carrying the team from Bahrain. Guards inside tried to close the gate, but they were outnumbered. In a tug of war over the gate, Mahboubeh Abbasgholizadeh's foot was crushed. The women made a big fuss and called an ambulance. The guards, embarrassed, at last let them in. The victory was sweet—especially since Iran won the game.

In April 2010, Reporters Without Borders again singled out Iran, this time awarding journalist Jila Bani Yaghoob the Freedom of Expression award for her blog *We Are Journalists*, which deals with the news in Iran, social issues, and women's lives. "Her career has been

In April 2006, Iran's President Ahmadinejad abruptly lifted the ban on Iranian women attending sports events. Having women at the games would promote better behavior among the sports fans, he said. In accordance with gender segregation policies, women and men would be seated in separate areas. Women's activists applauded. But hard-liners in the Iranian government soon forced Ahmadinejad to take back his order.

The white scarves resumed their campaign. Occasionally they got lucky. In February 2009, four protesters handed a letter explaining their plight to Korean women attending a soccer match between Iran and Korea at Azadi Stadium. "Could you please shout once, just once, for us in support of Iran?" the letter pleaded. "Could you do it for us, sisters?" The Korean women showed their solidarity by taking the Iranian women with them into the stadium.

marked by intimidation and abusive arrests intended to silence her," the citation said. "But she has never bowed to the constant pressure from the Iranian authorities." The same could be said of a remarkable number of Iranian women fighting for women's rights.

CHAPTER 9

A TIME OF
TURMOIL

"The highest ideals for women are freedom and putting an end to discrimination. This is not only specific to women of Iran, it is an ideal women across the world struggle for. In certain countries women have had more success in removing discrimination but we have not been successful. This is a reality."

—Zahra Rahnavard, Iranian university professor and leader of the Iranian prodemocracy Green Movement, March 2010

The widespread opposition to Ahmadinejad during his repressive first term gave hope to many Iranians that he could be defeated in 2009. Large numbers of women activists had stayed away from the polls in 2005 when Ahmadinejad won the presidency. They also stayed away in 2008 when the number of women deputies in the Majlis slipped down to eight. In the spring of 2009, a return to electoral politics seemed wise.

To take a united front on women's issues, forty-two women's groups and seven hundred individual activists formed a coalition called the Women's Convergence. They agreed to present the presidential candidates with two demands: the ratification of CEDAW and the revision of four articles in the constitution that discriminated against women. They did not specifically endorse any particular candidate, but asked each one to respond to their statement.

Their effort had a visible effect on the campaign. All three of the candidates running against Ahmadinejad promised to address the coalition's demands. They also said that, if elected, they would include women ministers in their cabinets. Even more amazing, they campaigned for election with their wives, a practice unheard of in the Islamic Republic.

The most active candidate's wife was Zahra Rahnavard, the wife

Zahra Rahnavard *(right)* accompanies her husband, presidential candidate Mir-Hossein Mousavi *(left)*, to a campaign event in Tehran in April 2009.

of Mir-Hossein Mousavi, the front-running reform candidate. She appeared frequently with her husband, sometimes holding his hand in public. She often gave campaign speeches for her husband, speaking out for women's rights. The other reform candidate, Mehdi Karroubi, also involved his wife in his campaign. He appointed a woman activist who had served in the sixth Majlis as spokesperson for his campaign. The wife of the conservative candidate Mohsen Rezai accompanied him to several campaign stops. Even President Ahmadinejad brought his wife to one event.

Iranians turned out in huge numbers on election day, June 12, 2009. Polls had to remain open until midnight to accommodate all the voters.

■ ■ ■ POST-ELECTION PROTESTS

The next day, when the election commission announced Ahmadinejad's victory before all the ballots were counted, millions of Iranians marched in protest. They waved green banners (green was the color of Mousavi's campaign) and challenged the official results with signs asking "Where Is My Vote?" Women, especially young women but also many older women activists, walked proudly at the front of the column or alongside the men. They didn't walk apart and behind them as women did in government-sponsored rallies. Emotions ran high. The first massive rally at Tehran's Azadi Tower on June 15 clogged streets for miles around. It was the largest street protest in Iran since the 1979 revolution.

Marches continued for more than two weeks. Supreme Leader Khamenei and the Guardian Council agreed to a recount. On June 29, after a recount of 10 percent of randomly selected ballots, Ahmadinejad was again declared the winner.

By then the protesters had consolidated into what they called the Green Movement. It is a nonviolent, prodemocracy movement for individual freedom and civil rights, including women's rights. Women from all walks of life, some in traditional chadors and others in bright green scarves, played a large part in the movement.

REPRESSION

Police, basijis, and security forces acted swiftly and harshly to repress the marches and the movement. Wielding batons and guns, they injured many demonstrators as well as bystanders. They arrested more than three thousand protesters. About sixty civilians lost their lives in the violence. Twenty-seven-year-old Neda Agha-Soltan was getting out of a car on her way to join a demonstration on June 20, 2009, when a basiji sniper shot her. Her death, recorded on a cell-phone camera and sent around the world, became an icon of the movement.

The tragic deaths of so many, mostly young people, inspired more demonstrations and outrage.

An Iranian opposition protester holds up a picture of Neda Agha-Soltan at a rally in December 2009. Agha-Soltan was killed on her way to a demonstration in June 2009.

A mother who searched Tehran's prisons for her nineteen-year-old son for three weeks finally found his body in the morgue. He had died while in the custody of the security forces. Daring to speak out about her ordeal, Parvin Fahimi united the mothers of other young activists killed by the regime. Every Saturday, the Mourning Mothers gathered in a park in Tehran to memorialize their lost children and to call for the release of political prisoners.

Prominent women's activists were among those arrested. Police detained Faezeh Hashemi briefly during the protests. In July 2009, journalist Shadi Sadr was on her way to Friday prayer when security forces seized her so roughly that she lost her headscarf and coat. While security agents held and interrogated her for eleven days in prison, other agents searched and took papers from her home and office.

AHMADINEJAD AND WOMEN'S ISSUES

Ahmadinejad's second inauguration took place on August 5, 2009, in spite of continued protests. In an apparent concession to the women's movement, he nominated three women to be ministers. All the nominees belonged to conservative parties. Two had served in the seventh Islamic Majlis (2004-2008), where they had supported policies that women's rights activists rejected as discriminatory. The third, however, was Marzieh Vahid Dastjerdi. As a two-term Majlis deputy (1992-2000), she had annoyed feminists with her proposal for gender-segregated health facilities and her opposition to CEDAW. But she did vote in

Marzieh Vahid Dastjerdi is the first female cabinet minister in the Islamic Republic of Iran. She was confirmed by the Majlis to be minister of health in 2009.

favor of women's custody rights and women advisory judges in courts dealing with family matters.

Of the three nominees, the Majlis confirmed only Dastjerdi. As minister of health, she became the first woman to head a ministry in the Islamic Republic. It was ironic that this milestone was brought about by a hard-line conservative president.

Ahmadinejad also appointed a woman vice president for science and technology. Neither appointment assured women's rights activists that Ahmadinejad would improve women's lives in Iran.

In spite of having appointed women to government posts, Ahmadinejad introduced policies that limited women's advancement. Gender segregation was again introduced into the universities, and women who wished to go to college were required to study at universities in their home cities or towns. Male students faced no such restrictions on where they could study. Quotas on college admissions further limited women's opportunities.

The Majlis passed a new "protection of family" bill. It gave a man further powers to remarry without the consent or even knowledge of his current wife.

■ ■ ■ TARGETING WOMEN ACTIVISTS

While the government sought to suppress the ongoing Green Movement protests, it also began a campaign directed against women's rights activists. Shirin Ebadi was a prime target. Ebadi had left Iran before the elections to attend a conference in Spain. She did not return.

In August 2009, the judiciary held a show trial of Ebadi and more than one hundred other human rights and opposition leaders, none of whom were present. All were accused of conspiring against the Islamic Republic. In the fall, authorities arrested and beat Ebadi's husband. He was later released. But the government revoked his passport so that he could not leave Iran to join his wife abroad. In November, under pretext of collecting unpaid taxes, authorities seized Ebadi's Nobel Peace Prize medal and froze her and her husband's bank accounts. In late December, security forces took her sister into custody and detained her for three weeks.

The regime also targeted founders of the One Million Signatures Campaign. They, along with numerous Iranian women's rights lawyers and women journalists and bloggers, were put under surveillance, interrogated, and detained. In December police arrested Mahboubeh Abbasgholizadeh as she was on her way to the funeral of an ayatollah who had supported the reform movement. Security forces even harassed the Mourning Mothers. In December 2009, police arrested twenty-nine of the women during their weekly gathering. In January 2010, more than one hundred police and basijis appeared in Laleh Park again and chased and grabbed the women. They forced thirty women into police vans. A seventy-five-year-old member of the group had to be taken to the hospital. A third crackdown on the group occurred in February.

After the disputed presidential election in 2009, protests by the Green Movement continued throughout the fall. Many demonstrations took place on special holidays, when the government held official rallies. On Quds Day (Jerusalem Day), a holiday started by Ayatollah Khomeini to show solidarity with the Palestinian people, and at the November 4 observance of the 1979 takeover of the U.S. Embassy in Tehran, competing rallies voiced pro- and anti-government feelings. On National Students Day on December 7, 2009, angry young people held vigils at universities across Iran. Security forces and basijis clashed with tens of thousands of opposition supporters at these demonstrations.

Iranian security forces on motorcycles surround opposition protesters during clashes between protesters and police in December 2009. Several protesters were killed in the clashes that month.

Arrests continued as well, and not just at public rallies. In October 2009, police raided a private home where a prayer ceremony for the release of political prisoners was being held. About sixty guests were arrested. They included the wives of many prominent reformist politicians held in jail since their arrests in June 2009.

At night protesters shouted *"Allahu akbar"* (God is great) from their rooftops, the only safe place to vent their opposition. It was an echo of the period before the revolution, when Iranians defied the shah by shouting their support of Ayatollah Khomeini from rooftops.

On December 19, 2009, Grand Ayatollah Montazeri, who supported the reformists, died. His funeral sparked protests against the government in cities across Iran. A week later was the holy day of Ashura. On this day, Shia Muslims mourn the martyrdom of Hussein, the grandson of the prophet Muhammad. Protesters marched on Ashura, waving green banners. During these events, police arrested fifteen thousand more protesters and reported thirteen deaths.

In June 2010, on the anniversary of the presidential election, a few protesters dared to engage in skirmishes with the police. Most Iranians have withdrawn from direct confrontations with the regime. The streets are heavily patrolled. Nevertheless, late at night, cries of *"Allahu akbar"* still float across the dark skies of Iran.

Many other less well-known women activists also faced arrest. According to Abbasgholizadeh, about six hundred women active in the women's movement were detained between June 2009 and March 2010. Most were released within a few days but warned they would be treated more harshly if they continued to take part in unauthorized rallies. Security agents held others for longer periods, often in solitary confinement, and interrogated them without allowing them access to lawyers.

Iranian women's rights activist Mahboubeh Abbasgholizadeh was detained by the Iranian government in 2004, 2007, and 2009 for her work for women's rights in Iran.

▪▪▪ FLEEING IRAN

Subjected to constant harassment, some activists went into hiding. Many women left Iran altogether. In December 2009, the UN reported that since June 2009, more than forty-two thousand Iranians had sought refugee

> "My generation wants its most basic needs such as freedom of expression and personal freedoms. We want to live, we do not want to face persecution for expressing our political opinion; as women we don't want to walk on the street with the constant horror that we could be intimidated for showing an inch of hair."
>
> —Narges Kalhor, a young Iranian filmmaker who fled to Germany, October 2009

status (permission to live in another country because of persecution in one's own country). Most crossed the border to neighboring Turkey, which does not require a visa for visitors from Iran.

Fatemeh Haghighatjoo, threatened with a prison sentence for criticizing Iran's court system, left Iran soon after her resignation from the Majlis. Parvin Ardalan, Shadi Sadr, and Mahboubeh Abbasgholizadeh also fled the political repression in their homeland. Many women journalists also left. They include Nazila Fathi, who writes for the *New York Times*.

The government attempted to stop many women from leaving. A number of members of the One Million Signatures Campaign had their passports revoked. In March 2010, officials stopped Simin Behbahani from flying to an International Women's Day event in Paris.

Fatimah Haghighatjoo *(center)* speaks with other demonstrators during a sit-in protest in Tehran in 2004. Haghighatjoo fled Iran in 2005.

WHAT WILL BECOME OF THE WOMEN'S MOVEMENT IN IRAN?

The crackdown has taken its toll on the women's movement in Iran. In a March 2010 interview, Mahboubeh Abbasgholizadeh called the situation critical. The network of the Iranian women's movement has broken up into smaller groups, she said, making it difficult to organize campaigns. "Everyone has paid a price. [Activists] are either in prison or have been forced to relocate; some of them are in refugee camps or banned from traveling abroad or have been dismissed from their jobs or universities where they were studying."

Abbasgholizadeh also pointed out that the Green Movement has taken over the women's movement. The horrendous human rights violations of the government have overshadowed its discriminations against women. As a result, many women's rights activists have become human rights activists. This is not a bad thing, she said, but it has sidelined women's demands for social and economic change.

Yet the struggle continues. Women activists exiled from Iran continue to engage global support for the movement and to promote dialogue between Iranian women inside and outside Iran.

In spite of heavy government filtering, websites remain the best means of communication. In February 2010, political chaos encouraged the hard-liners to try to push through laws easing restrictions on polygamy. *Change for Equality* managed to collect twelve hundred signatures on a petition opposing the amendments that year.

Within Iran, a whole new generation of young women has become politicized by the regime's suppression of civil rights. Well-educated and often unable to find work, these women have brought fresh, bold determination to the One Million Signatures Campaign, other women's rights campaigns, and the Green Movement.

If Ahmadinejad and the hard-liners prevail, individual civil rights and citizen participation in government may be entirely lost. In April 2010, the Iranian authorities suspended the two principal reformist political parties, banned a reformist newspaper, and sentenced three reformist politicians to six years in prison. Former president Khatami was prohibited from traveling abroad. In an unprecedented move,

Longtime Iranian women's rights activists Shirin Ebadi *(left)* and Simin Behbahani *(right)* continue to work for change in their country.

the Majlis voted to end its constitutional right to review regulations issued by the Guardian Council. The step increased the authority of the Supreme Leader and the officials he appoints, while reducing the power of elected representatives. Many fear that Iran could become a totalitarian state in which citizens have no rights.

Ebadi remains steadfast in her belief that peaceful defiance is the best response. Asked by a British reporter if she is in danger from the regime, she replied:

I've never been contacted by the regime directly. But they contacted my family and friends and said 'Wherever she is, we can get rid of her.' I don't take that threat seriously. If people want to do something they don't talk about it beforehand. Their main aim is to scare me off doing my work properly. Obviously, I don't want to make my enemies happy, so I continue with my work inside the law.

Whatever happens, it is clear that Iran's women will not give up easily.

1500: Shia Islam becomes the state religion of Iran.

1905–1906: The Constitutional Revolution brings parliamentary government to Iran.

1907: The first school for Muslim girls opens in Tehran.

1910: The first women's periodical in the Persian language is published.

1918: The first teachers' training college for women opens in Tehran.

1919: Girls' education becomes an official part of the public school system in Iran.

1921: Colonel Reza Khan seizes power in Iran.

1922–1932: The Patriotic Women's League pushes for equal pay and reform of marriage, divorce, and inheritance laws in Iran.

1925: Reza Khan takes the title of shah in the new Pahlavi dynasty (family of rulers).

1936: Reza Shah Pahlavi orders Iranian women to unveil. Twelve women became the first females to attend the university in Tehran.

1941: During World War II (1939–1945), the Allies occupy Iran and force Reza Shah to give up rule in favor of his son, Mohammad Reza.

1940s: Iranian women activists form independent organizations and publications to promote women's rights in Iran.

1949–1953: The struggle between Prime Minister Mohammad Mosaddeq and the shah over the issue of nationalizing Iran's oil leads to Mosaddeq's overthrow by the U.S. Central Intelligence Agency (CIA).

1950s: Women's organizations in Iran petition the shah for equal rights, legal status, and opportunities.

1963: The shah's White Revolution gives Iranian women the vote. Six women win seats in the Majlis, and the shah appoints two women to the Senate. Iranian clerics lead an uprising against the reforms.

1964: The shah orders the arrest and exile of Ayatollah Khomeini.

1966: The Iranian government forms the Women's Organization of Iran (WOI) and bans independent women's groups.

1967: WOI codrafts a bill that becomes the Family Protection Law.

1968: Farrokhru Parsa becomes minister of education and the first Iranian woman to hold cabinet rank.

1975: WOI secretary Mahnaz Afkhami becomes the first minister for women's affairs. The Majlis amends the Family Protection Law.

1978: Protests and rioting against the shah escalate throughout the year. Women take an active role in protest marches.

1979:

January–February The shah, Mohammad Reza Pahlavi, leaves Iran, and Khomeini returns. The Islamic Revolution is quickly victorious. A Revolutionary Council led by Khomeini rules Iran by decree.

March 8–12	Iranian women protest any official return to veiling.
April 1	A national referendum decides in favor of an Islamic republic.
April–July	The Revolutionary Council declares new laws for Iran based on conservative interpretations of Sharia law. Iranian Muslim feminists form the Women's Society of the Islamic Revolution (WSIR).
November 4	Students invade the U.S. Embassy in Tehran and take U.S. citizens working there hostage.
December 2	The Constitution of the Islamic Republic of Iran is ratified by a national referendum. Ayatollah Khomeini becomes the first Supreme Leader of the Islamic Republic of Iran.

1980:

March	Four women win seats in the first Majlis elections of the Islamic Republic.
June 28	Ayatollah Khomeini decrees that all women must veil in government offices.
July 5, 7	Women in Tehran march against the veil.
September 22	Iraq attacks Iranian air bases, starting the 8-year Iran-Iraq War.

1981: U.S. hostages held in the U.S. Embassy in Tehran are released on January 20.

1984: Ayatollah Khomeini rules that Iranian women can work outside the home "within the Islamic laws and regulations."

1985: Women are recruited to serve in Iran's Basij. A women's seminary (religious school) opens in Qom.

1987: The Women's Social and Cultural Council works for an end to restrictions on the fields women are allowed to study in Iran.

1988: Iran accepts a UN-mediated cease-fire in the Iran-Iraq War.

1989: Khomeini dies. Ali Khamenei becomes Supreme Leader.

1992: Shahla Sherkat launches *Zanan* (Women). Iran's judiciary allows women to serve as legal consultants in family courts.

1997: The Guardian Council blocks Iranian women from running for president. Women's votes help elect moderate Mohammad Khatami as Iran's president.

1999: Iranian women win 783 seats in local elections

2000: Reformists gain a majority in the Majlis and pass many laws favorable to women. The Guardian Council vetoes these laws.

2003: Shirin Ebadi receives the Nobel Peace Prize for her defense of human rights in Iran.

2005: On June 12, women's groups hold the first public women's demonstration in Iran since 1980. Hard-line conservative Mahmoud Ahmadinejad wins Iran's presidential election in July.

2006:

June 12 Police break up a women's demonstration in Tehran and arrest seventy participants.

August 27 Change for Equality launches the One Million Signatures Campaign for legal reform.

December Arrests begin of women and men collecting signatures for the campaign.

2007:

March 4 Thirty-three women are arrested at the trial of four women detained in the June 12, 2006, demonstration.

November Security forces arrest four Iranian women bloggers for promoting women's rights in Iran online.

2008:

January Censors in Iran shut down the feminist periodical *Women*.

December The Iranian government closes Shirin Ebadi's Center for the Defenders of Human Rights.

2009:

June–December President Ahmadinejad's contested reelection brings protests across Iran. Police and security forces violently suppress the pro-democracy Green Movement. Many women activists are among those arrested.

2010: The detentions and arrests of Iranian women activists, human rights lawyers, journalists, bloggers, and family members of Green Movement activists continue. The Majlis votes to curb women's marital rights.

Mahboubeh Abbasgholizadeh

(b. 1958) As a theology student in Tehran, Mahboubeh Abbasgholizadeh grew interested in feminist readings of the Quran. After graduating, she translated and published a number of feminist books and edited the women's studies journal *Farzaneh* (Wise Woman). During the late 1990s, when Iran's judiciary shut down many publications, she founded the Association of Women Writers and Journalists to help unemployed women in publishing find work. She also formed a training center to strengthen women's associations. She was active in the Women's Access to Public Stadiums Campaign, Stop Stoning Forever, and the Iranian Women's Charter. Security forces arrested and detained her in November 2004, March 2007, and December 2009. After her last release, she left Iran for Europe. There she continues to speak out against the regime's repression of human rights.

Mahnaz Afkhami

(b. 1941) Born in Kerman in south central Iran, Mahnaz Afkhami moved to Seattle, Washington, with her mother when she was thirteen. She attended high school and college in the United States. After returning to Iran in 1967, she taught English at National University, worked with Iran's delegation to the United Nations, and became secretary-general of the Women's Organization of Iran. Working for WOI, she traveled around Iran meeting women and finding out about their lives and needs. In 1975 she became Iran's first cabinet minister for women's affairs, and she led the revision of the Family Protection Law to improve women's legal rights. After the revolution in 1979, the Islamic regime took her home. She was put on a death list, charged with "sowing corruption on earth" and "warring with God." Forced into exile, Afkhami began working with women

activists around the world, especially in Muslim societies, to help
women become leaders in their communities. She has written
six books about and for women, established the Iranian Studies
Foundation and the Women's Learning Partnership, and served
on the boards of human rights organizations.

Marzieh Vahid Dastjerdi

(b. 1959) As the first woman to be appointed a minister in
the government since the Islamic Revolution, Marzieh Vahid
Dastjerdi broke through a major barrier. Dastjerdi, a conservative
who served twice in the Majlis, belonged to the Zainab Society,
which tried to influence Ahmadinejad to appoint women
ministers. Before accepting the nomination, however, Dastjerdi
visited the Supreme Leader's office to be sure that he was not
opposed to women ministers. Besides her Majlis experience,
Dastjerdi, a gynecologist and medical researcher, oversaw a
maternity hospital and served on the board of the government's
Family Planning Association. A firm believer in strict controls
on women's dress, she also believes women should be appointed
judges and given equal divorce and custody rights.

Shirin Ebadi

(b. 1947) Shirin Ebadi is the most widely known defender
of women's rights in Iran. She is also one of the few Iranian
women to have successfully survived the transition from the
Pahlavi regime to the Islamic Republic. She refused to leave her
homeland in spite of losing her position as a federal judge in
1980. Blocked from pursuing her career as a judge, she began
writing about law. Once allowed to practice law again in 1992,
she focused on the rights of women and children. Her mission
soon broadened to include all human rights. Donating her

talents to cases that highlighted the suffering caused by unjust laws, Ebadi became well known. Her outspoken articles on the unfairness of Iran's penal code brought charges of speaking against Islam. But Ebadi learned to defend herself by citing Islamic principles and earlier examples. Her knowledge of law, her avoidance of politics, and her discipline, determination, and confidence in the rightness of her struggle helped keep her going. Now living in the United Kingdom, she remains confident that: "The continuation of peaceful, legitimate request of the people will finally and eventually pave the path to democracy in Iran." She was awarded the Nobel Peace Prize in 2003.

Faezeh Hashemi

(b. 1962) The younger daughter of former president Ali Akbar Hashemi Rafsanjani, Faezeh Hashemi grew up loving sports and physical activity. She studied sports in college, taught physical education, and managed sports clubs. In 1996 her father, then president, took her on a six-nation tour in Africa, where she promoted Muslim women in sports. Women in sports formed part of her platform when she ran for the Majlis that year. As a deputy, however, she found Majlis politics frustrating. Her political career ended when she lost her seat in the next Majlis elections. Her bold entry into journalism with *Zan* (Woman), a women's daily newspaper, was halted by Iranian censors in less than a year. Her greatest contribution to women's rights in Iran has been getting Iranian women to exercise and giving Iran's women athletes a chance to compete internationally. Hashemi started the Islamic Countries Women's Sports Solidarity Games and has served as vice president of the Iranian Olympic Committee. In 1995 the United Nations Conference for Women, meeting in Beijing, China, recognized Hashemi as a leader in the promotion of women's sports. In June 2009, she was among the thousands of Iranians arrested for peacefully protesting the results of the presidential election.

Ayatollah Ruhollah Mousavi Khomeini

(1902–1989) Khomeini was a leading Shia scholar teaching in a seminary in the city of Qom in 1963. That year Mohammad Reza Shah announced his program of reforms known as the White Revolution. Opposed to provisions allowing women and non-Muslims to hold office, Khomeini persuaded several senior clerics to sign a law calling for a boycott of the referendum on the reforms. This act led to Khomeini's arrest, which sparked three days of rioting. The following year, renewed friction between the shah and Khomeini brought about Khomeini's exile. During his exile, Khomeini developed his ideas of a just and fair Islamic state overseen by clerics. When he returned to Iran in February 1979, he took control of the government. Over the next two years, he created the theocracy he had earlier envisioned. It cost thousands of lives and became a regime even more repressive than the shah's. Even so, when Khomeini died in 1989, millions of Iranians mourned the death of this charismatic leader.

Noushin Ahmadi Khorasani

(b. 1967) An English major at Tehran University, Noushin Ahmadi Khorasani became involved in women's rights as a student. She later joined the Women's Society against Environmental Degradation and the Society for the Defense of the Rights of Children, a group started by Shirin Ebadi. She also worked with Shahla Lahiji publishing feminist books. Khorasani was editor in

chief of the feminist journal *Jense Dovom* (The Second Sex) until
the courts banned it in 2001. She promoted women's history
with a popular calendar (also banned after several issues). Her
publications helped raise interest in women's issues in Iran. She
organized International Women's Day celebrations, founded
the Women's Cultural Center in 1999, and helped plan the
rallies in June 2005 and 2006 and the One Million Signatures
Campaign. She has written a book about the campaign. In March
2007, she was among the thirty-three women arrested while
demonstrating in front of the Tehran courthouse where four
women were being tried after being arrested at a women's rights
protest in June 2006.

Shadi Sadr

(b. 1974) A lawyer from Tehran, Shadi Sadr took up writing
about women's issues soon after earning her law degree in 1996.
When the judiciary closed down the newspapers she worked for,
she set up a website called *Women in Iran* and edited the *Meydaan*
(Women's Field) website. In 2004 she founded Institution
for a Better Life, a legal counseling center that gives free legal
advice to women, many of them victims of domestic and social
violence. She helped initiate the Stop Stoning Forever campaign
and a drive to extend citizenship and nationality rights to the
children born to Iranian women married to non-Iranian men.
In March 2007, she was among the thirty-three women arrested
for protesting the trial of women who were arrested while
protesting in Tehran in 2006. In July 2009, security forces seized
and abducted Sadr. Freed eleven days later, she fled Iran. She has
won awards for her work from the Netherlands, Poland, the U.S.
Department of State, and Amnesty International.

Shahla Sherkat

(b. 1956) A journalist with a feminist mission, Shahla Sherkat edited *Zan-e Ruz* (Today's Woman) from 1983 to 1991. She launched *Zanan* (Women) in 1992. With this magazine, she hoped for the freedom to choose articles from a wider range of opinions than the government-run *Today's Woman* allowed. For sixteen years, *Women* reported on women's achievements and problems, tackling taboo subjects (such as AIDS, abortion, and violence against women) while allowing men to voice their opinions of women's social roles. Both clerics and secular feminists contributed articles. Opponents, however, trashed the magazine's offices. Money was so tight that Sherkat once sold her cell phone to pay the women on her staff. She frequently had to defend *Women* and its writers in court. Sherkat's endorsement of Mohammad Khatami as the candidate for gender equality in 1997 played an important role in his surprise landslide victory. Sherkat was arrested in 2000 for attending a reformist congress in Berlin, Germany. In 2008 officials refused to renew *Women's* license to publish. Sherkat has received international awards for her courageous journalism.

activist: someone who works toward achieving political or social goals

ayatollah: a title meaning "sign of God" in Arabic. It is given to the foremost Islamic scholars in Shia Islam who are experts in Islamic law, ethics, or philosophy, and who teach in Islamic seminaries. Especially distinguished ayatollahs are given the title of grand ayatollah. Grand ayatollahs are also known as *marjas*.

Basij: an Iranian volunteer people's militia created and trained by the Revolutionary Guard in Iran. Members are called basijis.

bazaar: a market area with shops and stalls

boycott: a protest involving a refusal to participate, such as a refusal to buy certain items for political reasons or a refusal to vote in an election

censor: an official who examines publications, broadcasts, or other media for objectionable matter and deletes the matter or halts distribution or airing of the publication, broadcast, or film

chador: a long piece of cloth that some Muslim women wear to cover the head, arms, torso, and legs

democracy: a system of government in which citizens have a direct say through free elections and political representation

dowry: in Iran, a religiously required financial pledge made by the husband to the wife at the time of marriage. It may be redeemed by the wife at any time.

feminism: belief in the political, economic, and social equality of women and men

feminist: a person who supports women's rights or interests or an activity on behalf of women's rights or interests

hijab: in Iran, the covering of the head and all of the body, except for the face and hands. It is required of all women and girls from age nine onward.

Islamist: a member of a political movement to establish a government based on a conservative interpretation of Islam, in which religious laws would control all sectors of society

Majlis: the Iranian parliament, or legislature

marja: an Islamic title meaning "Source of Emulation (following as a guide)" that is given to the highest legal authorities in Shia Islam

minister: the head of a government ministry (department)

Muslim feminist: a person who believes that Islam supports women's legal and political rights but gives men and women different yet balanced social roles.

Muslim feminists in Iran generally accept Islamic dress codes for women and emphasize the social importance of motherhood and family. Some reject the term *feminist* for themselves because they believe feminism focuses too much on individual rights and creates conflicts between men and women.

Ramadan: the ninth month of the Islamic calendar, when Muslims fast from dawn until sunset. It is a time of prayer, charitable deeds, and religious reflection and worship. It celebrates the time when the prophet Muhammad first began receiving messages from God.

referendum (plural referenda): a popular vote on a specific issue

reformist: a program or person advocating changes to improve a political system

revolution: a sudden and radical change, such as the overthrow of a ruler or an established political system by the subjects of that ruler

Revolutionary Guard: a military organization founded by Ayatollah Khomeini in Iran in 1979

secular: concerning civil or nonreligious matters

shah: "king" in Persian. It is a commonly used shortened version of *shahanshah*, the title of Iranian rulers dating back to the Persian Empire (550–330 B.C.) and meaning "king of kings."

theocracy: a government by divine guidance or by officials regarded as divinely guided

Western: of or relating to European or American political and social culture

White Revolution: a program of reforms in Iran proposed by Mohammad Reza Shah in 1963 and adopted by referendum. One of the reforms granted Iranian women the right to vote.

4 Nareyeh Tohidi, "Women at the Forefront of the Democracy Movement in Iran," in *The International Journal of Not-for-Profit Law* 7:3 (June 2005), http://www.icnl.org/knowledge/ijnl/vol7iss3/art_3.htm (June 25, 2010).

6 Nazila Fathi, "Hundreds of Women Protest Sex Discrimination in Iran," *New York Times*, June 13, 2005, A8.

6 Mahsa Sherkaloo, "Iranian Women Take On the Constitution," *Middle East Report Online*, July 21, 2005. http://www.merip.org/mero/mero072105.html (April 25, 2010).

7 Ibid.

8 *Ma`ayeb al-Rejal*, 1895, ed. Hasan Javadi et al. (Chicago: The Historical Society of Iranian Women, 1992), 124–128; cited in Hamideh Sedghi, *Women and Politics in Iran: Veiling, Unveiling,and Reveiling* (Cambridge: Cambridge University Press, 2007), 25.

9 Badr ol-Moluk Bamdad, *From Darkness into Light: Women's Emancipation in Iran*, ed. and trans. F.R.C. Bagley (Hicksville, N.Y.: Exposition Press, 1977), 66.

10 Seyyed Mohammad Jamalzadeh, *Yeki Bud Yeki Nabud* (Tehran: n.p., 1954), 106–107; cited in Sedghi, 25.

11 Bamdad, 17.

14 *Khaterat*, 1914; *Crowning Anguish: Memoirs of a Persian Princess from the Harem to Modernity, 1884–1914*, ed. Abbas Amanat, trans. Anna Vanzan and Amin Neshati (Washington, DC: Mage Publishers, 1993), 138.

14 *Crowning Anguish*, 148.

14 Ibid., 146.

16 Ibid., 284.

17 Ibid., 285.

18 "Complaints of Women of Tehran to the Honorable Anjuman of Theology Students," *Musavat* (Tehran), March 22, 1908, no. 18, 5-6, cited in Janet Afary, *The Iranian Constitutional Revolution 1906–1911: Grassroots Democracy, Social Democracy, and the Origins of Feminism* (New York: Columbia University Press, 1996), 190.

21 *Ghanun* (Law) 3 (1899), 4; cited in Parvin Paidar, *Women and the Political Process in Twentieth-Century Iran* (New York: Cambridge University Press, 1995), 53.

21 Nazim ul Islam Kirmani, *Tarikh-i bidari-yi Iraniyan* (Tehran, 1346 [1967]), I, 121; cited in Mangol Bayat-Philipp, "Women and Revolution in Iran," in Lois Beck and Nikki R. Keddie, eds., *Women in the Muslim World* (Cambridge: Harvard University Press, 1978), 298.

22 Ibid.

23 M. Yaukacheva, "The Feminist Movement in Persia," *Central Asian Review* VII: 1 (1959), 75.

23 Ahmad Kasravi, *Tarikh Mashruteh Iran* I (Tehran: Amir Kabir, 1978), 180-182; cited in Paidar, 56.

24 Afary 1996, 189.

24 Bamdad, 46.

25 Letter to *Habl ol-Matin*, December 1906, cited in Roshanak Mansur, "Chehreye Zan Dar Jaraid Mashrutiat," in *Nimeye Digar* I:1 (Spring 1363 [1984]), 23; cited in Paidar, 55.

26 Z. L. Khatsrevin, *Persianka* (Moscow, 1928), 39; cited in Yaukacheva, 75.

26 *Muzakirat-i Majlis*, August 4, 1911; cited in Afary 1996, 203.

27 Bamdad, 36.

28 Ruth Frances Woodsmall, *Moslem*

Women Enter a New World (New York: Round Table Press, 1936), 364.

28 C. Colliver Rice, *Persian Women and Their Ways* (London: Seeley, Service and Co., Ltd, 1923), 38.

30 *Shukufah* 4 (January 20, 1916), 2–3; cited in Afsaneh Najmabadi, "Zanha-yi millat: Women Or Wives of the Nation?" *Iranian Studies* 26:1–2 (Winter-Spring 1993), 70–71.

32 Bamdad, 61.

33 Cited in Sedghi, 56.

33 Sheikholeslami, 97–98; cited in Sedghi, 56.

33 Cited in Sedghi, 56–57.

34 Mohammad Sadr-Hashemi, *Tarikh jaraed va majalat Iran* [The History of Persian Newspapers and Magazines], 4 (Esfahan: Dad, 1332/1953), 262; cited in Eliz Sanasarian, *The Women's Rights Movement in Iran: Mutiny, Appeasement, and Repression from 1900 to Khomeini* (New York: Praeger, 1982), 33.

34 *Alam-e Nesvan*, May 1930, 130; cited in Sanasarian, 34.

35 Bamdad, 64.

40 Ayramlu, Taj al-Muluk, *Khaterat-e Malekeh Pahlavi* (Tehran: Beh Afrin Press, 2001), 41; cited in Janet Afary, *Sexual Politics in Modern Iran* (Cambridge: Cambridge University Press, 2009), 155.

40 Bamdad, 95–96.

40 National Archives, American Legation Despatch 684, January 16, 1936; cited in Donald N.Wilbur, *Riza Shah Pahlavi: The Resurrection and Reconstruction of Iran 1878–1944* (Hicksville, New York: Exposition Press, 1975), 173–174.

40 *My Prison, My Home: One Woman's Story of Captivity in Iran* (New York: Ecco, 2009), 22.

41 Arzoo Osanloo, *The Politics of Women's Rights in Iran* (Princeton, N.J.: Princeton University Press, 2009), 22.

41 Ervand Abrahamian, *Iran Between Two Revolutions* (Princeton, N.J.: Princeton University Press,1982), 144.

41 Reza Baraheni, *The Crowned Cannibals: Writings on Repression in Iran* (New York: Vintage Books, 1977), 52.

42 "I Acknowledge Freedom in the Clothes of Duty," *Alam-e Nesvan* [Women's Universe] 5 (September 1932), 220; cited in Jasamin Rostam-Kolayi, "Expanding Agendas for the 'New' Iranian Woman," in *The Making of Modern Iran*, Stephanie Cronin, ed., (London: Routledge, 2003), 169.

43 Article 1169 of the Iranian Civil Code, cited in Paidar, 110.

44 Mohammad Golbon, *Naghd Va Siahat: Majmueh Maghalat Va Taghrirat Fatemeh Sayyah* [The collected writings of Fatemeh Sayyah] (Tehran: Entesharat Tus, 1354 [1975], 146; cited in Paidar, 127.

46 Paidar, 124.

46 Cited in Paidar, 132

46 Golbon, 144, cited in Paidar, 133.

48 Sattareh Farman-Farmaian with Dona Munker, *Daughter of Persia* (New York: Crown Publishers, 1992), 90.

49 Bahaeddin Pazargad, *Chronology of the History of Iran* (Tehran: Eshragi Bookshop, 1345 [1966]), 313; cited in Paidar, 145.

51 *Sahifeh Imam* [A Collection of Imam Khomeini's Works] (Tehran: Nashr-e asar-e emam, 1378 [1999]). I: 314; cited in G. R. Afkhami, *The Life and Times of the Shah* (Berkeley and Los Angeles: University of California Press, 2009), 247.

54 "An Interview with Mahnaz Afkhami," in G. R. Afkhami, ed., *Jam'eh dowlat va jonbesh-e zanan-e iran: 1342–1357* [Women, State, and Society in Iran: 1963 to 1978], (Bethesda, MD: Foundation for Iranian Studies, 2003), 49–50; cited in G.R. Afkhami, *The Life and Times of the Shah* (Berkeley and Los Angeles: University of California Press, 2009), 252.

55 Haleh Esfandiari, *Reconstructed Lives: Women and Iran's Islamic Revolution* (Baltimore: The John Hopkins University Press, 1997), 33.

56 Amnesty International, *Annual Report for 1975–75* (London: Amnesty International, 1975); cited in Ervand Abrahamian, *A History of Modern Iran* (Cambridge: Cambridge University Press, 2009), 157.

58 Ray Vicker, "Women in Iran Take To Streets in a Move To Preserve Rights," *Wall Street Journal*, March 12, 1979, 1.

60 *Keyhan* [newspaper], March 1979; cited in Azar Tabari and Nahid Yeganeh, eds., *In the Shadow of Islam: The Women's Movement in Iran* (London: Zed Press, 1982), 35.

60 Youssef M. Ibrahim, "Iran's 'New' Women Rebel at Returning to the Veil," *New York Times*, March 11, 1979, E2.

60 Ibid.

61 Ibid.

61 "Men Stone, Jeer Iran Feminists," *Los Angeles Times*, March 9, 1979, B2.

61 Ibrahim, *New York Times*, March 11, 1979, E2.

63 "Women Claim Iran Veil Victory," *Los Angeles Times*, March 13, 1979, B1, B10.

63 Homa Hoodfar and Shadi Sadr, "Can Women Act as Agents of a Democratization of Theocracy in Iran?" Final Research Report prepared for the project Religion, Politics and Gender Reality for the United Nations Research Institute for Social Development, Heinrich Böll Stiftung, October 2009, 9. Available online at www.unrisd.org (November 30, 2009).

63 "Women Claim Iran Veil Victory," *Los Angeles Times*, March 13, 1979, B10.

63 Gregory Jaynes, "Bazargan Goes to See Khomeini as Iran Rift Grows," *New York Times*, March 9, 1979, A1, A7.

63 Gregory Jaynes, "Iranian Women: Looking Beyond the Chador," *New York Times Magazine*, April 22, 1979, 38.

64 Ibid., 100.

64 Fred Halliday, "Mujahidin: 'We Are an Islamic Movement Separate from the Ruling Oligarchy,'" *Middle East Research and Information Project Reports* 86 (March–April 1980), 19.

64 Sanasarian, 128.

64 John Kifner, "Iran's Women Fought, Won, and Dispersed," *New York Times*, March 16, 1979. A6

65 Oriana Fallaci, "An Interview with Khomeini," *The New York Times Magazine*, October 7, 1979, 9.

65 *Ettelaat* (newspaper), September 19, 1979; cited in Abrahamian 2008, 168.

67 Tim Wells, *444 Days: The Hostages Remember* (San Diego, CA: Harcourt Brace Jovanovich, 1985), 161.

70 Shirin Ebadi, *Iran Awakening: A Memoir of Revolution and Hope*, with Azadeh Moaveni (New York: Random House, 2006), 49.

72 Doyle McManus, "Iranian Women Protest Decree on Head Scarves,"

Los Angeles Times, July 6, 1980, A4.

73 Tabari and Yeganeh, 237.

73 Ibid.

74 Doyle McManus, "Iranian Women Protest Decree on Head Scarves," A1.

74 Ibid., A4.

74 Ibid., A1.

76 "On Hejab," in Tabari and Yeganeh, 107.

76 Maryam Poya, *Women, Work and Islamism: Ideology and Resistance in Iran* (London: Zed Books, 1999), 74.

77 Pari Shaikh al-Islami, *Zanan-I Ruznamahnigar va Andishmand-I Iran,* (Tehran: Maz Graphics, 1972), 88–99; cited in Afary 1996, 187.

77 Sanasarian, 131.

78 "An Exile's Dream for Iran" (Khomeini interview published in *Le Monde*, May 6, 1978), in Ali Reza Nobari, ed. *Iran Erupts* (Stanford: Stanford University, Iran America Documentation Group, 1978), 13.

78 "The Question of Women" in Tabari and Yeganeh, 99.

78 Sanasarian, 135.

79 *Toloueh Zane Mosalman* (Tehran: Mahboubeh Publications, n.d.), 103; cited in Poya, 65.

79 *Ettelaat*, March 31, 1984; cited in Poya, 80.

83 Ibid., February 3, 1982; cited in Farah Azari, "The Post-Revolutionary Women's Movement in Iran," in *Women of Iran: The Conflict with Fundamentalist Islam*, ed. Farah Azari (London: Ithaca Press, 1983), 215.

83 Cited in Homa Hoodfar and Shahla Sadr, 20.

85 Robin Wright, *The Last Great Revolution* (New York: Alfred A. Knopf, 2000), 155.

86 "Shirin Ebadi Nobel Prize Speech," Voices Education Project (Seattle, Washington). http://www.voiceseducation.org/content/shirin-ebadi-nobel-prize-speech (April 10, 2010).

90 Amendment of Article 6, Section 4 (1998) of Press Law (1990); cited in Mehrangiz Kar, *Crossing the Red Line: The Struggle for Human Rights in Iran* (Costa Mesa, CA: Blind Owl Press, 2007), 201.

91 Statement in Majlis by Dr. Marzieh Vahid-Dastjerdi; cited in Kar 2007, 202.

91 "Female Members of the 5th Majlis Confront the Public," *Bad Jens: Iranian Feminist Newsletter*, March 13, 2000. http://www.badjens.com/firstedition/majlis.htm (March 20, 2010).

91 Elaine Sciolino, *Persian Mirrors: The Elusive Face of Iran* (New York: The Free Press, 2000), 111.

92 Ibid., "Teheran Journal: From the Back Seat in Iran, Murmurs of Unrest," *New York Times*, April 23, 1992, A4.

94 Shirin Ebadi, *Iran Awakening*, 111.

94 Jane Howard, *Inside Iran: Women's Lives* (Washington, DC: Mage Publishers, 2002), 76.

95 Philip Taubman, "The Courageous Women of Iran," *New York Times*, December 26, 1997, A38.

96 Geraldine Brooks, *Nine Parts of Desire: The Hidden World of Islamic Women* (New York: Anchor Books, 1995), 208.

97 *Iran Sports Pages*, February 27, 2010. http://www.iransportspress.com/news/48/ARTICLE/9871/2010-2-27.html (April 4, 2010).

98 Cited in Wright, 133.

99 Rebecca Barlow and Shahram Akbarzadeh, "Prospects for Feminism in the Islamic Republic of Iran," *Human Rights Quarterly* 30 (2008), 31.

99 "Special Report: Shorn of Dignity and Equality—Women in Iran" *The Economist*, 369: 8346 (October 18, 2003), 26.

100 Abrahamian 2008, 191.

101 Howard, 171.

101 Ibid.

103 Mehrangiz Kar, "Women and Civil Society in Iran," in *On Shifting Ground: Muslim Women in the Global Era*, ed. Fereshteh Nouraie-Simone (New York: Feminist Press at the City University of New York, 2005), 229.

104 Nazila Fathi, "Iranian Women Defy Authority to Protest Sex Discrimination," *New York Times*, June 13, 2005, A8.

106 "Female Members of the 5th Majlis Confront the Public," *Bad Jens: Iranian Feminist Newsletter*.

106 Ibid.

106 Ziba Mir-Hosseini, "Fatemeh Haghighatjoo and the Sixth Majlis: A Woman in Her Own Right," *Middle East Report* 233 (Winter 2004), 35.

106 Shadi Sadr, "Women's Gains at Risk in Iran's New Parliament," *Women's E-News*, June 9, 2004. http://www .onlinewomeninpolitics.org/ archives/04_0608_iran_wip.htm (April 20, 2010).

107 "Iran: Legislators Tell All," National Council of Resistance of Iran Women's Committee, September 16, 2005. http://iranncrwomen .org/content/view/30/27/ (April 10, 2010).

109 Translated by Shahla Haeri and cited in Shahla Haeri, "Women, Religion, and Political Agency," in *Contemporary Iran: Economy, Society, Politics*, ed. Ali Gheissari (Oxford: Oxford University Press, 2009), 136.

110 Nayereh Tohidi, "Women at the Forefront."

111 Mahsa Sherkaloo, "Iranian Women Take On the Constitution."

111 Kaveh Ehsani, "Iran: The Populist Threat to Democracy," *Middle East Report* 241 (Winter, 2006), 8.

111 Hooman Majd, *The Ayatollah Begs to Differ: The Paradox of Modern Iran* (New York: Doubleday, 2008), 103.

112 Fatemeh Sadeghi, "Foot soldiers of the Islamic Republic's 'Culture of Modesty,'" *Middle East Report* 250 (Spring 2009), 51.

112 Ibid.

114 Iran Press Service, "Police Used Extreme Brutality Against Hundreds of Iranian Women," March 10, 2006. http://www .iran-press-service.com/ips/ articles-2006/march-2006/ women_day_10306.shtml (June 29, 2010).

115 Golnaz Esfandiari "Iran: Police Forcibly Disperse Women's Rights Protest in Tehran," *Radio Free Europe/Radio Liberty*, June 13, 2006. http://www.rferl.org/ articleprintview/1069121.html (April 15, 2010).

117 Noushin Ahmadi Khorasani, "Signed with an X," *New Internationalist* 398 (March 2007). http://www.newint.org/ features/2007/ 03/01/womens _rights/ (April 15, 2010).

117   Farangis Najibullah, "Iran:
       Women's Activist Wins
       Human Rights Award,"
       *Radio Free Europe/Radio
       Liberty*, February 14, 2008,
       http://www.rferl.org/
       articleprintview/1079477
       .html (April 15, 2010).

119   Nazila Fathi, "Iranian
       Women Are Arrested After
       Protests Outside Court," *New
       York Times*, March 6, 2007,
       A11.

119   "Women Will Not Be
       Silenced," *Interview Rooz* 1150,
       November 14, 2007. http://
       www.roozonline.com/
       english/interview/interview/
       article/2007/november/14/
       women-will-not-be-silenced
       .html (April 15, 2010).

119   "Iran: Six-Month Prison
       Sentences for Four Cyber-
       Feminists," *Reporters Without
       Borders*, September 4, 2008.
       http://en.rsf.org/iran-six
       -month-prison-sentences
       -for-04-09-2008,28410.html
       (April 17, 2010).

120   Afary 2009, 6.

122–123 "Iranian Journalist Jila Bani
       Yaghoob wins 'Freedom of
       Expression' Award Sponsored
       by *Reporters Without Borders*,"
       Reporters without Borders,
       April 15, 2010, http://en.rsf
       .org/iran-iranian-journalist
       -jila-bani-15-04-2010,37030
       .html (April 18, 2010).

123   "Where Are Our Iranian
       Sisters?" *Women's Field*,
       February 14, 2009. http://
       www.meydaan.com/English/
       showarticle.aspx?arid=759
       (June 25, 2010)

124   "New Year's (Nooroz)
       messages from the
       opposition," *Payvand*, March
       10, 2010. http://www
       .payvand.com/news/10/
       mar/1180.html (March 19,
       2010).

132   Nazila Fathi, "Iran's Politics
       Open a Generational Chasm,"
       New York Times, October 22,
       2009, A10.

134   "Abbasgholizadeh:
       Suppression Has Changed
       Iranian Women's Priorities,"
       International Campaign for
       Human Rights in Iran, March
       12, 2010. http://www
       .iranhumanrights
       .org/2010/03/
       abbasgholizadeh-suppression-
       has-changed-iranian-
       womens-priorities/ (April 7,
       2010).

135   Angus McDowall, "Shirin
       Ebadi's Interview with The
       Sunday Telegraph," *Sunday
       Telegraph* (London) February 6,
       2010. http://www.telegraph
       .co.uk/news/worldnews/
       middleeast/iran/7169398/
       Shirin-Ebadis-interview-with
       -The-Sunday-Telegraph.html
       (April 22, 2010).

143   "Lecture with Dr. Shirin
       Ebadi," Vancouver Canada,
       April 23, 2010, video and
       translation arranged by Dave
       Siavashi of *Iran News Now*,
       http://vimeo.com/11301643
       (May 4, 2010).

SELECTED BIBLIOGRAPHY

Abrahamian, Evrand. *A History of Modern Iran*. Cambridge, UK: Cambridge University Press, 2008.

Afary, Janet. *The Iranian Constitutional Revolution 1906–1911: Grassroots Democracy, Social Democracy, and the Origins of Feminism*. New York: Columbia University Press, 1996.

———. *Sexual Politics in Modern Iran*. Cambridge, UK: Cambridge University Press, 2009.

Ahmadi Khorasani, Noushin. *Iranian Women's One Million Signatures Campaign for Equality: The Inside Story*. Bethesda, MD: Women's Learning Partnership Translation Series, 2009.

Bamdad, Badr ol-Moluk. *From Darkness into Light: Women's Emancipation in Iran*. Edited and translated by F. R. C. Bagley. Hicksville, NY: Exposition Press, 1977.

Beck, Lois, and Guity Nashat, eds. *Women in Iran from 1800 to the Islamic Republic*. Urbana: University of Illinois Press, 2004.

Ebadi, Shirin. *Iran Awakening: A Memoir of Revolution and Hope*. With Azadeh Moaveni. New York: Random House, 2006.

Keddie, Nikki R. *Modern Iran: Roots and Results of Revolution*. New Haven, CT: Yale University Press, 2006.

———. *Women in the Middle East: Past and Present*. Princeton, NJ: Princeton University Press, 2007.

Paidar, Parvin. *Women and the Political Process in Twentieth-Century Iran*. New York: Cambridge University Press, 1995.

Poya, Maryam [Elaheh Rostami-Povey]. *Women, Work and Islamism: Ideology and Resistance in Iran*. London: Zed Books, 1999.

Sanasarian, Eliz. *The Women's Rights Movement in Iran: Mutiny, Appeasement, and Repression from 1900 to Khomeini*. New York: Praeger, 1982.

Sedghi, Hamideh. *Women and Politics in Iran: Veiling, Unveiling, and Reveiling*. Cambridge, UK: Cambridge University Press, 2007.

Change for Equality. http://www.we-change.org/english/ This website of the One Million Signatures Campaign carries news of the ongoing drive to teach women about gender inequality in Iranian law and sign a petition for legal reform, as well as archives of past events.

Esfandiari, Haleh. *My Prison, My Home: One Woman's Story of Captivity in Iran.* New York: Ecco, 2009. Esfandiari gives both a moving account of her ordeal in Evin Prison in Evin, Iran, in 2007 and a clear explanation of Iran's history and culture.

Farman Farmaian, Sattareh, and Dona Munker. *Daughter of Persia: A Woman's Journey from Her Father's Harem through the Islamic Revolution.* New York: Crown Publishers, 1992. Farman Farmaian's memoirs vividly portray life in Iran in the twentieth century.

Iranian Women March against Hijab on March 8, 1979. 10 minutes. http://www.youttube .com/watch?v=odmlfa986mk This video of a historic demonstration captures the issues that women faced during the transition to Islamism in Iran in the 1970s, 1980, 1990s, and 2000s.

January, Brendan. *The Iranian Revolution.* Minneapolis: Twenty-First Century Books, 2008. This book explains the roots of the 1979 revolution in Iran and presents the showdown between Iran and the United States during the hostage crisis.

Kar, Mehrangiz, and Kim Longinotto. *Divorce Iranian Style.* 1998. http://video.google .com/videoplay?docid=7607777740102230188# This documentary film offers a fly-on-the-wall look at several weeks in an Iranian divorce court.

Kort, Michael E. *The Handbook of the Middle East* (rev. ed.) Minneapolis: Twenty-First Century Books, 2008. This book includes the history, geography, and social customs of the countries of the Middle East, accompanied by maps, a who's who section, and a timeline.

Moaveni, Azadeh. *Lipstick Jihad.* New York: Public Affairs, 2005. An Iranian American from California writes of her experiences in Iran as a reporter for *Time* magazine.

Satrapi, Marjane. *The Complete Persepolis.* New York: Pantheon, 2007. This memoir, written and illustrated in graphic novel style, captures Satrapi's childhood experiences of the 1979 Islamic Revolution in Iran and the hardships of living in exile.

Taus-Bolstad, Stacy. *Iran in Pictures.* Minneapolis: Twenty-First Century Books, 2004. This book in the Visual Geography Series focuses on the geography, history, and social customs of Iran.

Women Living under Muslim Laws. http://www.wluml.org/ An international network, Women Living under Muslim Laws provides information about and for women whose lives are affected by various forms of Islamic law.

PHOTO ACKNOWLEDGMENTS

The images in this book are used with the permission of: REUTERS/Raheb Homavandi PJH/AH, p. 5; AP Photo/Arshia Kiani, pp. 6, 110; © Christine Spengler/Sygma/ CORBIS, p. 10; © Unknown/Brooklyn Museum/CORBIS, p. 15; © Laura Westlund/ Independent Picture Service, p. 19; © W & D Downey/Hulton Archive/Getty Images, p. 21; Everett Collection, p. 27; © Transcendental Graphics/Archive Photos/Getty Images, p. 34; © De Agostini Picture Library/Getty Images, p. 36; AP Photo, pp. 47, 50, 57 (both), 62, 66, 115; © Popperfoto/Getty Images, p. 48; © Dimitri Kessel/ Time Life Pictures/Getty Images, p. 53 (top); © Paul Popper/Popperfoto/Getty Images, p. 53 (bottom); © Gabriel Duval/AFP/Getty Images, p. 59; © Atta Kenare/ AFP/Getty Images, pp. 67, 112; © Imagestate Media Partners Limited-Impact Photos/ Alamy, p. 69; © Bettmann/CORBIS, p. 73; © Mahmoudreza Kalari/Sygma/CORBIS, p. 74; © Kaveh Kazemi/Hulton Archive/Getty Images, pp. 74-75, 76, 79; © AFP/Getty Images, pp. 82 (left), 93, 127, 128, 130; © Kaveh Kazemi/Getty Images, p. 82 (right); © Thomas Hartwell/Time & Life Pictures/Getty Images, p. 87; © Jean Michel Cadiot/AFP/Getty Images, p. 90; © Doug Pensinger/Getty Images, p. 96; AP Photo/ Mohammad Sayyad, p. 97; AP Photo/John McConnico, p. 103; AP Photo/Hasan Sarbakhshian, pp. 105, 132; © Henghamen Fahimi/AFP/Getty Images, pp. 108, 133; AP Photo/Henrik Montgomery, p. 121 (top); © Vince Bucci/Getty Images, p. 121 (bottom); © Roshan Norouzi/ZUMA Press, p. 125; © Caren Firouz/Reuters/CORBIS, p. 135.

Front cover: © Roshan Norouzi/ZUMA Press.

ABOUT THE AUTHOR

Diana Childress has written ten books and scores of magazine articles for children and young adults, mainly on historical topics. Recent published titles include *Omar al-Bashir's Sudan*, *Johannes Gutenberg and the Printing Press*, and *Barefoot Conquistador*, a biography of the sixteenth-century Spanish explorer Álvar Núñez Cabeza de Vaca. She lives in New York City.